I KNOW WHY THE CAGED BIRD SINGS

Maya Angelou

Introduction: Stopping to Buy SparkNotes on a Snowy Evening

Whose words these are you *think* you know.
Your paper's due tomorrow, though;
We're glad to see you stopping here
To get some help before you go.

Lost your course? You'll find it here.
Face tests and essays without fear.
Between the words, good grades at stake:
Get great results throughout the year.

Once school bells caused your heart to quake
As teachers circled each mistake.
Use SparkNotes and no longer weep,
Ace every single test you take.

Yes, books are lovely, dark, and deep,
But only what you grasp you keep,
With hours to go before you sleep,
With hours to go before you sleep.

Contents

CONTEXT

MAYA ANGELOU WAS BORN Marguerite Anne Johnson on April 4, 1928, in St. Louis, Missouri. Her older brother, Bailey Johnson, Jr., could not pronounce her name when he was little, so he called her Mya Sister, then My, which eventually became Maya. When Angelou was three years old, her parents divorced and sent their children to live in the rural, segregated town of Stamps, Arkansas, with their paternal grandmother, Annie Henderson. During their teens, they lived with their mother, Vivian Baxter, in California. At the age of fifteen, Angelou began her career as a civil-rights activist of sorts. She battled racism with dogged persistence and succeeded in becoming the first African American hired to the position of streetcar conductor in San Francisco.

Angelou has remained a civil-rights activist throughout her life. At Dr. Martin Luther King, Jr.'s request, Angelou became the northern coordinator for the Southern Christian Leadership Conference in the 1960s. Presidents Gerald Ford and Jimmy Carter also respected her leadership qualities. Ford appointed her to the American Revolutionary Bicentennial Advisory Commission, and Carter appointed her to the National Commission on the Observance of the International Woman's Year. At President Bill Clinton's request, she wrote and delivered a poem, "On the Pulse of Morning," for his 1993 presidential inauguration, becoming only the second poet in American history to receive such an honor.

Maya Angelou's work in the arts includes writing, film, and theater. She moved to New York and earned a role in the Gershwin opera *Porgy and Bess*. Along with the rest of the cast, she toured nearly two-dozen countries in Europe and Africa from 1954 to 1955. After marrying a South African freedom fighter, Angelou lived in Cairo, Egypt, for several years, where she edited an English-language newspaper. Later, she taught at the University of Ghana and edited the *African Review*.

Angelou often shared stories about her unusual, intense, and poignant childhood, and her friends and associates encouraged her to write an autobiography. In 1969, Angelou published *I Know Why the Caged Bird Sings*, the first in a series of autobiographical works. It quickly became a best-seller and was nominated for the National

Book Award. Angelou's *Georgia, Georgia* became the first original screenplay by a black woman to be produced and filmed. *Just Give Me a Cool Drink of Water 'fore I Die,* a collection of poetry, was nominated for the Pulitzer Prize. Angelou was also nominated for an Emmy award for her performance in the film adaptation of Alex Haley's *Roots.* By 1995, she had spent two years on *The New York Times* Paperback Nonfiction Bestseller list, becoming the first African American author to achieve such success.

Out of her five autobiographies, *I Know Why the Caged Bird Sings* is probably Angelou's most popular and critically acclaimed volume. The book is now frequently read as a complement to fictional works that delve into the subject of racism, such as Harper Lee's *To Kill a Mockingbird* and Ralph Ellison's *Invisible Man.* It has often been cut from reading lists because it involves honest depictions of Angelou's sexuality and her experience of being raped as a child. She wrote *I Know Why the Caged Bird Sings* at a time when autobiographies of women, and particularly black women, had begun to proclaim women's significance in the mainstream as thinkers and activists. Angelou's book conveys the difficulties associated with the mixture of racial and gender discrimination endured by a southern black girl. At the same time, she speaks to many other issues, such as the relationships between parents and children, child abuse, and the search for one's own path in life.

Plot Overview

I N *I Know Why the Caged Bird Sings,* Maya Angelou describes her coming of age as a precocious but insecure black girl in the American South during the 1930s and subsequently in California during the 1940s. Maya's parents divorce when she is only three years old and ship Maya and her older brother, Bailey, to live with their paternal grandmother, Annie Henderson, in rural Stamps, Arkansas. Annie, whom they call Momma, runs the only store in the black section of Stamps and becomes the central moral figure in Maya's childhood.

As young children, Maya and Bailey struggle with the pain of having been rejected and abandoned by their parents. Maya also finds herself tormented by the belief that she is an ugly child who will never measure up to genteel, white girls. She does not feel equal to other black children. One Easter Sunday, Maya is unable to finish reciting a poem in church, and self-consciously feeling ridiculed and a failure, Maya races from the church crying, laughing, and wetting herself. Bailey sticks up for Maya when people actually make fun of her to her face, wielding his charisma to put others in their place.

Growing up in Stamps, Maya faces a deep-seated southern racism manifested in wearying daily indignities and terrifying lynch mobs. She spends time at Momma's store, observing the cotton-pickers as they journey to and from work in the fields. When Maya is eight, her father, of whom she has no memory, arrives in Stamps unexpectedly and takes her and Bailey to live with their mother, Vivian, in St. Louis, Missouri. Beautiful and alluring, Vivian lives a wild life working in gambling parlors. One morning Vivian's live-in boyfriend, Mr. Freeman, sexually molests Maya, and he later rapes her. They go to court and afterward Mr. Freeman is violently murdered, probably by some the underground criminal associates of Maya's family.

In the aftermath of these events, Maya endures the guilt and shame of having been sexually abused. She also believes that she bears responsibility for Mr. Freeman's death because she denied in court that he had molested her prior to the rape. Believing that she has become a mouthpiece for the devil, Maya stops speaking to everyone except Bailey. Her mother's family accepts her silence at first as temporary post-rape trauma, but they later become frustrated and angry at what they perceive to be disrespectful behavior.

To Maya's relief, but Bailey's regret, Maya and Bailey return to Stamps to live with Momma. Momma manages to break through Maya's silence by introducing her to Mrs. Bertha Flowers, a kind, educated woman who tells Maya to read works of literature out loud, giving her books of poetry that help her to regain her voice.

During these years in Stamps, Maya becomes aware of both the fragility and the strength of her community. She attends a church revival during which a priest preaches implicitly against white hypocrisy through his sermon on charity. The spiritual strength gained during the sermon soon dissipates as the revival crowd walks home past the honky-tonk party. Maya also observes the entire community listening to the Joe Louis heavyweight championship boxing match, desperately longing for him to defend his title against his white opponent.

Maya endures several appalling incidents that teach her about the insidious nature of racism. At age ten, Maya takes a job for a white woman who calls Maya "Mary" for her own convenience. Maya becomes enraged and retaliates by breaking the woman's fine china. At Maya's eighth grade graduation, a white speaker devastates the proud community by explaining that black students are expected to become only athletes or servants. When Maya gets a rotten tooth, Momma takes her to the only dentist in Stamps, a white man who insults her, saying he'd rather place his hand in a dog's mouth than in hers. The last straw comes when Bailey encounters a dead, rotting black man and witnesses a white man's satisfaction at seeing the body. Momma begins to fear for the children's well-being and saves money to bring them to Vivian, who now lives in California.

When Maya is thirteen, the family moves to live with Vivian in Los Angeles and then in Oakland, California. When Vivian marries Daddy Clidell, a positive father figure, they move with him to San Francisco, the first city where Maya feels at home. She spends one summer with her father, Big Bailey, in Los Angeles and has to put up with his cruel indifference and his hostile girlfriend, Dolores. After Dolores cuts her in a fight, Maya runs away and lives for a month with a group of homeless teenagers in a junkyard. She returns to San Francisco strong and self-assured. She defies racist hiring policies in wartime San Francisco to become the first black streetcar conductor at age fifteen. At sixteen, she hides her pregnancy from her mother and stepfather for eight months and graduates from high school. The account ends as Maya begins to feel confident as a mother to her newborn son.

CHARACTER LIST

Maya Angelou (Marguerite Ann Johnson) Maya Angelou—named Marguerite Ann Johnson at birth—writes about her experiences growing up as a black girl in the rural South and in the cities of St. Louis, Los Angeles, and San Francisco. Maya has an unusual degree of curiosity and perceptiveness. Haunted by her displacement from her biological parents and her sense that she is ugly, Maya often isolates herself, escaping into her reading. Angelou's autobiography traces the start of her development into an independent, wise, and compassionate woman.

Bailey Johnson, Jr. Maya's older brother. Like Maya, he is intelligent and mature beyond his age. Though Bailey enjoys sports and fares well in social situations, he also shows deep compassion for his isolated sister. Bailey senses the negative influences of racism, but to protect himself from despair, he chooses to anesthetize himself and subdue his soul until the negative moment passes.

Annie Henderson (Momma) Maya and Bailey's paternal grandmother. Momma raises them for most of their childhood. She owns the only store in the black section of Stamps, Arkansas, and it serves as the central gathering place for the black community. She raises the children according to stern Christian values and strict rules. Though she never reacts with emotion, both children feel her love anyway.

Vivian Baxter Bailey and Maya's mother. Although she has a nursing degree, she earns most of her money working in gambling parlors or by gambling herself. Though Vivian and Momma have very different values, they are both strong, supportive women. A somewhat inattentive mother, Vivian nevertheless treats her children with love and respect.

Big Bailey Johnson Maya and Bailey's father. Despite his lively personality, he is handsome, vain, and selfish. He stands out among the other rural blacks because of his proper English and his flashy possessions. Maya implies that Big Bailey's pretensions result from his disenfranchisement as a black man in the United States. Big Bailey does not respect, care for, or connect with Maya.

Willy Johnson Momma's son, who is in his thirties. Crippled in a childhood accident, Uncle Willy lives his entire life with Momma. He suffers insults and jokes because of his disability. Like Momma, he is a devout Christian, and he acts as the children's disciplinarian and protector.

Daddy Clidell Vivian's second husband, whom she marries after her children join her in California. Although Maya initially tries to dismiss him, Daddy Clidell becomes the only real "father" Maya knows. He combines the virtues of strength and tenderness and enjoys thinking of himself as Maya's father. He introduces her to his con-men friends and teaches her how to play poker. A successful businessman despite his lack of education, he remains modest and confident.

Mr. Freeman Vivian's live-in boyfriend in St. Louis. When Maya and Bailey move to St. Louis, Mr. Freeman sexually molests and rapes Maya, taking advantage of her need for physical affection and her innocent, self-conscious nature. In retrospect, Maya feels partly responsible for Mr. Freeman's fate, and her guilt over his murder haunts her throughout her childhood.

Mrs. Bertha Flowers A black aristocrat living in Stamps, Arkansas. One of Maya's idols, she becomes the first person to prod Maya out of her silence after Maya's rape, taking an interest in Maya and making her feel special. Maya respects Mrs. Flowers mainly for encouraging her love of literature.

Mrs. Viola Cullinan A Southern white woman in Stamps and Maya's first employer. Perhaps unwittingly, she hides her racism under a self-deceptive veneer of gentility. Mrs. Cullinan's disrespect for Maya's wish to be called by her given name leads to Maya's subtly rebellious smashing of the Cullinans' china.

Glory (Formerly Hallelujah) Mrs. Cullinan's cook. A descendent of the slaves once owned by the Cullinan family, her acceptance of Mrs. Cullinan's condescending and racist renaming practices contrasts with Maya's resistance.

Mr. Edward Donleavy A white speaker at Maya's eighth-grade graduation ceremony. He insults the black community by talking condescendingly, but not explicitly, of their limited potential in a racist society. His racist tone casts a pall over the graduation and infuriates Maya.

Henry Reed The valedictorian of Maya's eighth-grade graduating class. He leads the class in "Lift Ev'ry Voice and Sing," popularly known as the Black National Anthem, and renews his community's pride following Mr. Donleavy's speech. This moment catalyzes Maya's great pride in her heritage and also inspires her passion for black poets and orators.

Dolores Stockland Big Bailey's prim-and-proper live-in girlfriend in Los Angeles. Maya spends the summer with them when she is fifteen and drives Dolores into a jealous rage. Maya's decision to show compassion toward her shows Maya's capacity for mercy, despite her self-aware and proud nature.

Louise Kendricks Maya's first friend outside her family. When she is with Louise, Maya is able to escape her troubles and play like a child should.

Tommy Valdon An eighth-grader who writes Maya a valentine. Maya reacts with hostility at first, distrusting any man's advances after the rape. She softens when Tommy writes her another letter showing that his interest in her is sincere.

Joyce Bailey's first love, with whom he loses his virginity. Joyce's relationship with Bailey foreshadows the troubles associated with adolescent sexuality that Maya will experience in San Francisco. Four years older than Bailey, Joyce turns his innocent displays of sexual curiosity playing "Momma and Papa" into sexual intercourse and eventually runs away with a railroad porter whom she meets at the store, leaving Bailey heartbroken and morose.

Dr. Lincoln A white dentist in Stamps to whom Momma lent money during the Great Depression. Momma's staunch effort to appeal to his sense of ethics to support her in treating Maya's tooth shows both her resolve and her ability to act somewhat unethically out of necessity. The scene also reinforces Maya's impression of Momma as a superhero.

Stonewall Jimmy, Spots, Just Black, Cool Clyde, Tight Coat, and Red Leg Daddy Clidell's con-men friends, who teach Maya that it is possible to use white prejudice to gain advantage over whites. They represent creativity and the ethics that result from necessity and desperation.

Mrs. Florida Taylor Mr. Taylor's wife of forty years. Maya attends Florida's funeral and confronts her own mortality for the first time.

Miss Kirwin Maya's teacher in San Francisco. Miss Kirwin treats Maya like an equal human being, regardless of her color.

ANALYSIS OF MAJOR CHARACTERS

MARGUERITE ANN JOHNSON (MAYA)

At the beginning of *I Know Why the Caged Bird Sings*, Maya is a precocious young girl suffering not just from the typical traumas associated with being black and female in America, but also from the trauma of displacement. Smart and imaginative, Maya nevertheless feels that people judge her unfairly due to her ungainly appearance. Feeling misunderstood, she fantasizes that she is a blond-haired, blue-eyed girl trapped in a "black ugly dream" and will soon wake up and reveal her true self. Maya describes her social and familial displacement as "unnecessary insults" on top of the general difficulties associated with growing up as a black girl in the segregated American South. The South presents Maya with three tremendous impediments: white prejudice, black powerlessness, and female subjugation.

In addition to these broad societal obstacles, Maya endures many personal traumas in her lifetime as well. Her parents abandon her and Bailey when Maya is three, and her sense of abandonment and her need for physical affection lead to further struggles. Five years later, she must leave the only home she has known and live in an unknown city where she seeks comfort in Mr. Freeman, who molests and rapes her. At age ten, having already witnessed callous whites mistreating the people she loves most, such as Momma, Maya begins to experience racism directly. Mrs. Cullinan tries to rename and demean her, and the racist, white dentist Dr. Lincoln says he would rather stick his hand in a dog's mouth than treat Maya's problem. In San Francisco, Maya's confusion about sexuality becomes compounded when she becomes pregnant at age sixteen.

Angelou's autobiography documents her victories and successes as well. With Bailey's and Momma's unwavering love and later encouragement from Vivian, Daddy Clidell, and numerous role models and friends, Maya gains the strength to overcome difficulties and realize her full potential. She learns to confront racism actively and eventually secures a position as the first black conductor aboard a San Francisco streetcar, which is perhaps her crowning achievement in the book. She also learns to confront her own failings with dignity and honor, never forgetting her guilt about lying in court and, in the Los Angeles junkyard, realizing the need to think not just in terms of black and white, but in terms of humanity in all its diversity. She shows the power of forgiveness as she tries to find positive qualities in Big Bailey and to show compassion toward Dolores. She remains insecure, especially about her sexuality and appearance, but eventually she learns to trust her own abilities, as we see in the final scene, when she realizes that she will be able to care for her newborn son.

BAILEY JOHNSON JR.

Maya's older brother by one year, Bailey is the most important person in Maya's life throughout her childhood. When moved around from place to place, Bailey and Maya depend on each other to achieve some semblance of stability and continuity in their lives. Unlike Maya, Bailey is graceful, attractive, outgoing, and charming, and many consider him the jewel of his family. Bailey uses his skills and status to protect Maya. With his charms, he defends her against criticism and insults. Bailey and Maya share not just in tragedies but also in private jokes and a love of language and poetry.

One of the most striking differences between Maya and Bailey is their ability to confront racism. Bailey explains to Maya early on that when he senses the negative effects of racism, he essentially puts his soul to sleep so that he can forget the incident. Maya, however, learns to resist racism actively. Bailey and Maya grow further apart as they go through adolescence, and Bailey continues to withdraw deeper into himself. Even so, Maya continues to confide in him, asking for advice about her pregnancy. He continues to show his love for her as well, replying quickly to his sister and giving caring advice.

The return to Stamps from St. Louis traumatizes Bailey, and though he never blames his sister, he remains tormented by his longing for his mother. He expresses his longing through moodiness, sarcasm, and a bold assertion of his independence. In Stamps, he finds outlets for his longing for maternal affection by watching the white movie star who looks like Vivian and by playing "Momma and Papa" with Joyce, his buxom girlfriend who is four years his senior. In San Francisco, Bailey tries to win his mother's approval by imitating the people she befriends—he becomes the pimp-like boyfriend of a white prostitute. Bailey moves out at age sixteen and gets a job on the Southern Pacific Railroad, explaining that he and Vivian have come to an understanding with each other and that he has grown wise beyond his years.

ANNIE HENDERSON (MOMMA)

Maya and Bailey's paternal grandmother, Momma raises them for most of their childhood. She owns the only store in the black section of Stamps, Arkansas, and it serves as the central gathering place for the black community. She has owned the store for about twenty-five years, starting it as a mobile lunch counter and eventually building the store in the heart of the black community. Not knowing that Momma was black, a judge once subpoenaed her as "Mrs. Henderson," which cemented her elevated status in the mind of the black community.

Similarly, Momma is the moral center of the family and especially of Maya's life. Momma raises the children according to stern Christian values and strict rules. She is defined by an unshakable faith in God, her loyalty to her community, and a deep love for everything she touches. Despite the affection she feels for her grandchildren, she cares more about their well-being than her own needs, extracting them from the Stamps community when the racist pressures begin to affect Bailey negatively.

While in Stamps, Momma teaches Maya how to conduct herself around white people. She chooses her words, emotions, and battles carefully, especially when race plays a role. Momma considers herself a realist regarding race relations. She stands up for herself but believes that white people cannot be spoken to without risking one's life. When three nasty poor white children mock Momma from the yard one afternoon, Maya watches furiously, but Momma maintains her dignity by not even acknowledging their taunts. Though stern and not given to emotional or affectionate displays, Momma conveys the depth of her love for Maya and Bailey throughout the book.

VIVIAN BAXTER

Although she has a nursing degree, Maya and Bailey's mother earns her money working in gambling parlors. Vivian's parents and brothers are tough city dwellers who thrive in St. Louis amid the chaos of Prohibition, and Vivian seems to have inherited the family's wild streak. Though her lifestyle differs greatly from that of Momma, Vivian is also strong, proud, practical, and financially independent. She is also devastatingly beautiful—it is fitting that Maya and Bailey discover a white actress with a striking likeness to their mother because to them Vivian appears as a goddess performer who exists in her own personal spotlight. Maya is dumbstruck by Vivian's magnetic beauty and Bailey falls in love with her at first sight. Maya believes Vivian initially sent them away because Vivian was, in Maya's opinion, too gorgeous to have children.

Vivian always treats Maya and Bailey well, and it is hard to imagine that she would have sent them so far away as young children. At the same time, however, even when they live together, the children remain peripheral to Vivian's life. Even after living together for some time and growing closer, Maya notes that Vivian notices Maya not out of the corner of her eye but "out of the corner of her existence." Showing her practical nature, Vivian sees no need to focus attention on Maya as long as Maya is healthy, well-clothed, and at least outwardly happy.

Throughout the book, Vivian oscillates between her gifts and limitations as a parent. In St. Louis, Vivian does not realize the danger of leaving her young daughter at home with a man who spends all day pining and waiting for her to come home. She does, however, demonstrate a high degree of maternal intuition when her live-in boyfriend, Mr. Freeman, sexually molests and rapes Maya. Without even knowing what has happened, Vivian kicks him out of the house immediately. Later, however, she proves unable to deal with Maya's post-rape trauma, and Maya and Bailey go back to Stamps. Similarly, in San Francisco, Vivian's lifestyle prevents her from actively engaging her daughter about Maya's sexuality, leading indirectly to Maya's pregnancy. Even so, when Maya becomes pregnant, Vivian supports and encourages her without condemnation, and it is Vivian who gives Maya her first and most important lesson about trusting her maternal instincts. Maya admires Vivian's unflinching honesty, strength, and caring nature, despite her frequent fumbling as a parent.

BIG BAILEY JOHNSON

Maya and Bailey's father exemplifies ignorant, parental neglect. He is handsome and vain, and he speaks with proper English, almost to the point of caricaturing a stereotypical, upper-class white man of the time. Big Bailey ruins his own attempts to reconnect with his children, particularly with Maya. Absent from the children's lives for years, he arrives in Stamps out of the blue one year, impressing the children and everyone else in town with his congenial nature and his fancy car and clothing, but Maya feels neither glad nor sad to see him go when they reach St. Louis. She regards him as a stranger, for he shows little genuine effort to care for her.

Though he resurfaces at the end of the book when Maya is fifteen and living in California, Big Bailey has not changed. Maya learns more about him—that he lives in a trailer park and suffers from many of the same troubles that afflict other black men trying to advance in the world—but he fails to try to learn anything about Maya. Even though Maya enjoys seeing her father's jubilant spirit in Mexico, the harsh reality of his selfishness continually undermines his appeal.

When first presenting him in the book, Maya questions whether Big Bailey obtains his possessions legally as a railroad porter or whether he advances through illegal means. At that point, he exemplifies the ethics of necessity seen elsewhere in the book, in which blacks compromise ethical behavior to break through the walls of racial injustice. Later, regardless of his methods, he exemplifies the tragedy of the American black man trying to advance in a white society obsessed with class, paying more attention to his image than to his family.

THEMES, MOTIFS & SYMBOLS

THEMES

Themes are the fundamental and often universal ideas explored in a literary work.

RACISM AND SEGREGATION

Maya confronts the insidious effects of racism and segregation in America at a very young age. She internalizes the idea that blond hair is beautiful and that she is a fat black girl trapped in a nightmare. Stamps, Arkansas, is so thoroughly segregated that as a child Maya does not quite believe that white people exist. As Maya gets older, she is confronted by more overt and personal incidents of racism, such as a white speaker's condescending address at her eighth-grade graduation, her white boss's insistence on calling her Mary, and a white dentist's refusal to treat her. The importance of Joe Louis's world championship boxing match to the black community reveals the dearth of publicly recognized African American heroes. It also demonstrates the desperate nature of the black community's hope for vindication through the athletic triumph of one man. These unjust social realities confine and demean Maya and her relatives. She comes to learn how the pressures of living in a thoroughly racist society have profoundly shaped the character of her family members, and she strives to surmount them.

DEBILITATING DISPLACEMENT

Maya is shuttled around to seven different homes between the ages of three and sixteen: from California to Stamps to St. Louis to Stamps to Los Angeles to Oakland to San Francisco to Los Angeles to San Francisco. As expressed in the poem she tries to recite on Easter, the statement "I didn't come to stay" becomes her shield against the cold reality of her rootlessness. Besieged by the "tripartite cross-fire" of racism, sexism, and power, young Maya is belittled and degraded at every turn, making her unable to put down her shield and feel comfortable staying in one place. When she is thirteen and moves to San Francisco with her mother, Bailey, and Daddy Clidell, she feels that she belongs somewhere for the first time. Maya identifies with the city as a town full of displaced people.

Maya's personal displacement echoes the larger societal forces that displaced blacks all across the country. She realizes that thousands of other terrified black children made the same journey as she and Bailey, traveling on their own to newly affluent parents in northern cities, or back to southern towns when the North failed to supply the economic prosperity it had promised. African Americans descended from slaves who were displaced from their homes and homelands in Africa, and following the Emancipation Proclamation in 1862, blacks continued to struggle to find their place in a country still hostile to their heritage.

RESISTANCE TO RACISM

Black peoples' resistance to racism takes many forms in *I Know Why the Caged Bird Sings*. Momma maintains her dignity by seeing things realistically and keeping to herself. Big Bailey buys flashy clothes and drives a fancy car to proclaim his worth and runs around with women to assert his masculinity in the face of dehumanizing and emasculating racism. Daddy Clidell's friends learn to use white peoples' prejudice against them in elaborate and lucrative cons. Vivian's family cultivates toughness and establishes connections to underground forces that deter any harassment. Maya first experiments with resistance when she breaks her white employer's heirloom china. Her bravest act of defiance happens when she becomes the first black streetcar conductor in San Francisco. Blacks also used the church as a venue of subversive resistance. At the revival, the preacher gives a thinly veiled sermon criticizing whites' charity, and the community revels in the idea of white people burning in hell for their actions.

MOTIFS

Motifs are recurring structures, contrasts, or literary devices that can help to develop and inform the text's major themes.

STRONG BLACK WOMEN

Though Maya struggles with insecurity and displacement throughout her childhood, she has a remarkable number of strong female role models in her family and community. Momma, Vivian, Grand mother Baxter, and Bertha Flowers have very different personalities and views on life, but they all chart their own paths and manage to maintain their dignity and self-respect. None of them ever capitulates to racist indignities.

Maya also charts her own path, fighting to become the first black streetcar conductor in San Francisco, and she does so with the support and encouragement of her female predecessors. Maya notes at the end of Chapter 34 that the towering character of the black American woman should be seen as the predictable outcome of a hard-fought struggle. Many black women fall along the way. The ones who can weather the storm of sexism and racism obviously will shine with greatness. They have survived, and therefore by definition they are survivors.

LITERATURE

Maya's first love is William Shakespeare. Throughout her life, literature plays a significant role in bolstering her confidence and providing a world of fantasy and escape. When feeling isolated in St. Louis, she takes refuge in the library. She describes Mrs. Bertha Flowers as being like women in English novels. Mrs. Flowers helps Maya rediscover her voice after her rape by encouraging her to use the words of other writers and poets. Maya continually quotes and refers to the literature she read throughout her childhood. For instance, at one point she simply gives San Francisco the title "Pride and Prejudice" without referring specifically to Jane Austen's novel of the same name. Bailey appreciates Maya's love of literature. He often presents her with gifts, such as the book of Edgar Allen Poe's work that he and Maya read aloud while walking in their backyard in Stamps.

NAMING

Maya's real name is Marguerite, and most of her family members call her Ritie. The fact that she chooses to go by Maya as an adult, a name given to her by her brother, Bailey, indicates the depth of love and admiration she holds for him. When Maya reunites with her mother and her mother's family in St. Louis at age eight, one of her uncles tells her the story of how she got this name. Thus, finding her family is connected with finding her name and her identity. Indeed, for African Americans in general, Maya notes, naming is a sensitive issue because it provides a sense of identity in a hostile world that aims to stereotype blacks and erase their individuality and identity.

MOTIFS

Consequently, given the predominance of pejoratives like *nigger* so often used to cut down blacks, Maya notes the danger associated with calling a black person anything that could be loosely interpreted as insulting. Besides the obvious fact that Mrs. Cullinan does not take the time to get Maya's name right in the first place, Mrs. Cullinan wishes to manipulate Maya's name for her own convenience, shortening it to Mary, illustrating that she cares very little about Maya's wishes or identity. Maya becomes enraged, and the incident inspires her to commit her first act of resistance.

SYMBOLS

> *Symbols are objects, characters, figures, or colors used to represent abstract ideas or concepts.*

THE STORE

Momma's store is a central gathering place in Stamps and the center of Maya's childhood. There she witnesses the cycles of nature and labor, tending to workers in the cotton-picking season and canners during the killing season. Maya notes that until she left Arkansas for good at age thirteen, the Store was her favorite place to be. It symbolizes the rewards of hard work and loyalty and the importance of a strong and devout community.

MAYA'S EASTER DRESS

The lavender taffeta dress that Momma alters for Maya on Easter symbolizes Maya's lack of love for herself and her wish for acceptance through transformation. She believes that beauty means *white* beauty. Hanging by the sewing machine, the dress looks magical. Maya imagines that the dress will reveal her true self to people who will then be shocked by her beauty. Harsh reality strikes on Easter morning, however, when she realizes that the dress is only a white woman's throwaway that cannot wake her from her black nightmare. Maya learns that her transformation will have to take place from within.

Summary & Analysis

Chapters 1–5

Summary: Untitled Prologue

If growing up is painful for the Southern Black girl,
being aware of her displacement is the rust on the
razor that threatens the throat.

(See QUOTATIONS, p. 51)

A young black girl named Maya stands in front of her church congregation on Easter, unable to finish reciting a poem. She wears an unflattering altered taffeta dress that, she notes, is probably a secondhand dress from a white woman, and she fantasizes that one day she will wake up out of her "black ugly dream" and be white and blond instead of a large, unattractive African American girl. After being humiliated in front of everyone and tripped by another child, she ends up running out of church peeing, crying, and laughing all at the same time.

Summary: Chapter 1

Prior to this incident, when Maya is three years old and her brother, Bailey, is four, their parents divorce. Their parents send the children by train with a porter from California to Stamps, Arkansas, to live with their paternal grandmother, Annie Henderson, and her disabled adult son, Willie. The porter abandons the children the next day in Arizona, and the two young children make the rest of the trip to Stamps with pieces of paper tacked on their bodies listing their final destination. Mrs. Henderson, whom the children soon begin to call Momma, owns and runs the only store in the black section of Stamps. The Store is the center of the community, and Momma is one of the community's most respected residents.

During the cotton-harvesting season, Momma awakes at four in the morning to sell lunches to the crowd of black cotton laborers before they begin the day's grueling work. In the morning, the laborers appear full of hope and energy, but by the end of the day, they barely have enough energy to drag themselves home. They always earn less than they thought they would, and they often voice suspicions about illegally weighted scales. The stereotype of happy, singing cotton pickers enrages Maya. The laborers never earn enough to pay their debts, much less enough to save a penny.

SUMMARY: CHAPTER 2
Willie, who was crippled in a childhood accident, acts as the children's disciplinarian. Willie becomes the butt of jokes in the community, in part due to his handicap, but also because he lives a relatively stable life while most able-bodied black men can barely support themselves. Maya returns home from school one day to see him, for the first time, hiding his handicap from two strangers who have stopped briefly at the Store. Maya understands and sympathizes with the tiring pity and contempt Willie must feel, and the incident makes her feel closer to him. During this time, Maya falls in love with reading, especially William Shakespeare, though she feels a bit guilty because Shakespeare was a white man.

SUMMARY: CHAPTER 3
One afternoon, Mr. Steward, the white former sheriff, comes to warn Momma that the whites are on the warpath because they say a black man has "messed with" a white woman. Momma hides Willie in the potato and onion bins in case the mob comes to the store looking for a scapegoat to lynch. Luckily it does not, but Maya clearly notes Willie's moans coming from the bins.

SUMMARY: CHAPTER 4
As a child, Maya constantly hears from others that she is ugly. She has kinky hair and dark skin, and she is large for her age. Bailey, on the other hand, is a small, graceful and attractive child. Whenever somebody remarks on Maya's ugly appearance, Bailey makes sure to avenge his sister by insulting the offending party. Maya considers Bailey the most important person in her world.

SUMMARY: CHAPTER 5
Momma insists that the children observe rules and respect their elders. The only children who do not respect Momma are poor white children. It pains Maya to hear them disrespect Momma and Willy by addressing them by their first names. One day, when Maya is ten, three poor white children approach the Store. Momma sends Maya inside. The children mock Momma by mimicking her stance

and gestures and Maya cries with impotent rage. Meanwhile, Momma says nothing and simply hums gospel hymns. One of the older white girls does a handstand, and her dress falls over her head revealing that she wears no underwear. Maya is furious, but when Momma enters the Store, Maya realizes that Momma has somehow fought and won a battle with the white children.

ANALYSIS: CHAPTERS 1–5

The lines from the poem Maya cannot finish, "What are you looking at me for? I didn't come to stay . . ." capture two of the most significant issues she struggles with in her childhood and young adulthood: feeling ugly and awkward and never feeling attached to one place. First, Maya imagines that though people judge her unfairly by her awkward looks, they will be surprised one day when her true self emerges. At the time, she hopes that she will emerge as if in a fairy-tale as a beautiful, blond white girl. By the age of five or six, Maya has already begun to equate beauty with whiteness, a sign that the racism rampant in the society in which she grows up has infiltrated her mind. Second, uprooted and sent away from her parents at age three, Maya has trouble throughout her life feeling that she belongs anywhere or that she has "come to stay." Her sense of displacement may stem in part from the fact that black people were not considered full-fledged Americans, but primarily she feels abandoned by her family. When she and Bailey arrive in Stamps, the note posted on their bodies is not addressed to Annie Henderson, but rather "To Whom It May Concern."

The opening scene in the church introduces these important issues while also conveying the frustration, humiliation, disillusionment, and, finally, liberation that define Maya's childhood. The childish voice interspersed throughout Angelou's adult reflections suggests that she is probably five or six years old at the time of the opening scene. Maya does not anchor her prologue in a specific time, suggesting that she continues to experience the emotions of this episode over and over again throughout her life. The prologue ends with an unforgettable description that Angelou uses to foreshadow the nature of the story to come. She says that growing up as a black girl in the South is like putting a razor to one's throat, but, even worse, when that black girl feels alienated from her own black community, her sense of displacement is like the rust on the razor, making life even more unbearable. She says that her displacement is "an unnecessary insult." Since the opening scene shows that Angelou was aware of her displacement, she prepares us to witness a childhood full of such extra insults. Nevertheless, it is significant that Maya manages to escape the critical, mocking church community and laugh about her liberation, even though she knows that she will be punished for it. Maya's escape foreshadows her eventual overcoming of the limitations of her childhood.

Maya's experiences in the Store ("Store" is capitalized by Angelou) tell much about black rural small-town life during the 1930s. After the Civil War and after they had been promised land and animals with which to farm, blacks in the South entered into a period of American history nearly as discriminatory and violent as the period of slavery. The post-Reconstruction era, known as the Jim Crow era, witnessed the systematic destruction of the black farmer in the South at the hands of resentful whites who sought to undermine the black entitlement to property, animals, financial support, or even wages. The Jim Crow era also brought with it severe segregation laws that affected every walk of life and spurred the development of white racist organizations, such as the Ku Klux Klan, which terrorized black communities. Positioned in the Store at the center of the community, Maya vividly and poignantly describes the cotton pickers' plight, describing their beleaguered bodies, their torn clothes, and their wearied faces when returning from the fields. Moreover, though Stamps is so thoroughly segregated that, as a child, Maya feels she hardly knows what white people look like, the social and economic effects of segregation profoundly affect Maya, her family, and her experiences. Maya recounts Mr. Steward's warning of the white lynch mob as an example of the conflicted nature of many whites' acts of kindness toward blacks. According to Maya, however, his casual attitude toward the terrorization of the black community destroys any virtue his gesture might indicate. Even Willie, whom he deems "innocent," has to hide in a potato bin all night while the white men scour the black section of Stamps for a scapegoat.

Against the backdrop of such terrifying events, Momma keeps her faith and self-respect, providing an influential example for Maya and Bailey. Her confrontation with the three white girls—another example of the overt insidiousness of racism—becomes a victory for Momma because she refuses to be displaced. While Maya feels apprehension, Momma's refusal to retreat inside the Store at their approach diffuses any threat the children pose to her authority or her identity. Under her silent, impassive gaze, their antics become an embarrassment to *them,* not to Momma. Momma addresses the girls with respect, demonstrating her maturity and poise. She shows that, though these girls may be above her on the social ladder, she is better and stronger than they are. In the context of the girls' ridiculous and terrible behavior, a level to which Momma never stoops herself, Momma's respectful address becomes ironic. From the beginning, Maya shows that Momma and Bailey—her hero who sticks up for her time and time again—provide her with a loving, respectful foundation that will support her in the future.

CHAPTERS 6–10

SUMMARY: CHAPTER 6
Reverend Howard Thomas, the presiding church elder in the district, visits Stamps every three months. He stays with Momma on Saturday and delivers a sermon in church on Sunday. Maya and Bailey hate him because he always eats the best parts of Sunday dinner.

SUMMARY: CHAPTER 7
Momma does not believe it is safe for black people to speak to whites and certainly not with insolence. She does not speak too harshly of whites even in their absence unless she generically refers to whites as "they." Maya says that Momma would have called herself a realist rather than a coward. Once, a black man accused of assaulting a white woman took refuge in Momma's Store. He eventually left, only to be apprehended later. In court, he testified that he had stayed with Mrs. Henderson. The judge subpoenaed Mrs. Henderson only to realize to his surprise that the accused had referred to a black woman as "Mrs." This unusual title, usually reserved for whites, indicates Momma's high status in her community.

SUMMARY: CHAPTER 8

> *A light shade had been pulled down between the*
> *Black community and all things white, but one could*
> *see through it enough to develop a fear-admiration-*
> *contempt . . .*   (See QUOTATIONS, p. 52)

One Christmas, Maya and Bailey's parents send them gifts. The children go outside and cry, wondering what they did wrong to be sent away in the first place. Having convinced themselves that their mother was dead, they find it hard to imagine that she could "laugh and eat oranges in the sunshine without her children." Momma admonishes them for being ungrateful. Later, Maya and Bailey destroy the blond, blue-eyed China doll their mother sent.

SUMMARY: CHAPTER 9

Big Bailey, the children's father, comes to visit Stamps a year later unexpectedly. He owns a car, and he speaks like a white man. His height and his handsome features astound Maya. He stays in Stamps for three weeks before surprising the children with the news that he will drive them to St. Louis to see their mother. Momma seems sad, but she simply tells the children to behave well. Maya cannot believe that Big Bailey is her father and she regards him as a complete stranger. Her brother, Bailey, jokes and laughs easily with Big Bailey.

When the children see their mother for the first time, Vivian's beauty strikes Maya dumb, and Bailey falls in love with her. Maya surmises that the intensity of Bailey's feelings stems from the fact that he and his mother resemble each other in physical beauty and personality. When Big Bailey leaves for California a few days later, Maya feels indifferent because she considers him a stranger who has now left her with another stranger.

SUMMARY: CHAPTER 10

Having landed in St. Louis during the heyday of Prohibition, Bailey and Maya meet all kinds of underground organized crime figures. Vivian's mother, Grandmother Baxter, entertains these men, and she has influence with the police. Vivian's brothers have city jobs, positions rarely held by black men, and they have a reputation for meanness, beating up on both whites and blacks. Maya stands in awe of her uncles, whom she describes as mean, though never cruel. They treat the children well and share stories about them as toddlers, even telling Maya how she got her nickname. When Bailey was less than three years old he learned that Maya, whose birth name is Marguerite, was his sister, and he began calling her "Mya sister" and then simply "My," which later morphed into "Maya." Uncle Tommy even tells Maya that she should not worry about not being pretty, because she is smart. Bailey and Maya live with their maternal grandparents for six months before moving in with Vivian and her older, fat boyfriend, Mr. Freeman, who feels insecure about his relationship with Vivian. The shift in location does not affect Maya, who never feels like she belongs anywhere. She feels that she and Bailey have been fated to live differently from other children.

ANALYSIS: CHAPTERS 6–10

Momma's philosophy regarding the safest way to deal with whites typifies the attitudes prevalent during the Jim Crow era—the period between 1877 and the mid-1960's during which a strict racial caste system relegated blacks in the South to the position of second-class citizens. Lynch mobs represented only one danger faced by American blacks in the rural South. Segregation became more than a physical reality since it influenced the culture and the mind-set of the black population as well. Specific comments about particular people could prove dangerous if those comments reached the wrong ears. Some people might have called Momma a coward, Maya acknowledges, but she adds that Momma would have called herself a realist. Momma survived the odds stacked against her and became a successful businesswoman. She saved the Store in the Great Depression while many white businesses failed all over the country. In Angelou's autobiography, Momma emerges as a strong, determined survivor. Momma chooses her battles well. For example, although Momma does not go out of her way to confront whites and their racism, she offers her help to those who find themselves mired in such confrontations. She and Willie aid a black man fleeing from a lynch mob despite the danger such actions might present to themselves, revealing their quiet bravery. Angelou remarks that when Momma reveals herself as the "Mrs. Henderson" subpoenaed by the judge, whites considered the incident a joke, but the black community remembered the incident as a testimony to Momma's stature.

Angelou's memory of Big Bailey reveals that he stands completely out of place in the rural South. She remarks that he wears tight clothes made of wool and that he pronounces English even better than the school principal. His behavior indicates that he tried hard to make a big impression. His brashness upset the quiet balance of routine in Momma's family. His car, his accent, and his clothing were all marks of middle-class status, but he worked as a porter in a California hotel. Angelou never says whether Big Bailey acquired his possessions by saving his wages or by other, perhaps illegal means. Indeed, intelligent black men with goals and aspirations in Big Bailey's generation had few legal avenues to use to achieve success. In what is known as the Great Migration, between one and two million black farmers left the South from 1914 to 1930 in search of work in northern cities, where factory owners promised but never provided high-wage jobs. The black migration from the rural countryside to the cities divided blacks from their heritage and their roots, stranding them in a world where, it seemed, one had to look, talk, and act white in order to succeed.

Despite her re-location to the loud, exotic, chaotic, and alien city of St. Louis, to a certain extent Maya shows her ability to engage with her new environment. She does not find true happiness in her relationship with her mother, but she meets a host of strong-willed and idiosyncratic relatives who begin to improve her attitude about herself. She remembers that one of her uncles continually tells her not to worry about her appearance but rather to cherish her intelligence. Moreover, Maya can now place herself in a larger familial context and learn a little about what her life was like before she was sent away, including endearing, love-affirming stories about her brother, Bailey. She learns that, as a three-year-old, Bailey took responsibility for teaching his sister how to walk.

Maya's Grandmother Baxter was nearly white and was raised by a German family. She married a black man but chose not to pass as white, and she achieved financial success and security by connecting with the criminal underworld. Maya's grandfather and uncles are rough city folk who have cultivated a necessary toughness that wards off abuse and exploitation, and her mother's exotic lifestyle seems to fit right in with Maya's unusual family. Despite the lack of familiarity, Maya has landed in a more familial world where, she says, she feels a need to appreciate her benefactors and fears being returned to Stamps. She soon learns that she has not adjusted well and that the family she meets in St. Louis practices criminal behavior, which affects her personally.

CHAPTERS 11–15

SUMMARY: CHAPTER 11

Maya shields herself against the confusion of St. Louis by reading fairy-tales and telling herself that she does not intend on staying there anyway. Vivian works in a gambling parlor at night. Maya pities Mr. Freeman because he spends his days at home waiting for Vivian to return. Maya begins sleeping at night with Vivian and Mr. Freeman because she suffers from nightmares. One morning after Vivian has left the bed and the house, Mr. Freeman sexually molests Maya. He does not rape her but rather masturbates on the bed while holding her close to him. Afterward, he threatens to kill Bailey if Maya ever tells anyone, but Maya, who does not understand what has happened and who actually enjoyed being held by someone, cannot understand what caused such a threat. For weeks, Mr. Freeman ignores her, and then molests her again. Again, he ignores her for weeks. Maya feels rejected and hurt, but she loses herself in other things, such as books. She wishes she were a boy because the heroes in all her favorite books and stories are male. Bailey welcomes the move to St. Louis and he makes friends, with whom he plays baseball. Maya, however, does not make any friends during this time. She and Bailey begin to grow apart, so she spends her Saturdays in the library reading fantastic adventures.

SUMMARY: CHAPTER 12

In late spring, after Vivian stays out all night one time, Mr. Freeman sends Maya to buy milk. When she returns from the errand, Mr. Freeman rapes her. He threatens to kill her if she screams, and he threatens to kill Bailey if she tells anyone. Afterward, Mr. Freeman sends her to the library, but Maya returns home because of the intense physical pain she feels between her legs. She hides her underwear under her mattress and goes to bed. Vivian thinks she might be coming down with the measles. Later that night, Maya hears Vivian argue with Mr. Freeman. In the morning, Vivian tells Maya that Mr. Freeman has moved out. When Bailey tries to change the linens, the bloodied panties Maya has hidden under the mattress fall out.

SUMMARY: CHAPTER 13

Vivian takes Maya to the hospital. Bailey privately urges Maya to name the rapist, assuring her that he would not allow the culprit to kill him. Maya reveals Mr. Freeman's name, the authorities promptly arrest him. Maya thinks of herself as a grown woman, remembering that her nurses told her that she has already experienced the worst that life has to offer.

Maya feels caught in a trap when the attorney asks her whether there were any sexual incidents with Mr. Freeman prior to the rape. She fears rejection from her family if she admits to the previous incidents, but she does not want to lie either. Ultimately, she lies to the court and Mr. Freeman receives a sentence of one year and one day in prison. Surprisingly, he is temporarily released after the hearing, and a white policeman visits later that night to tell Grandmother Baxter that Mr. Freeman has been beaten to death. Maya hears them quickly drop the subject and briefly discuss casual matters before the policeman leaves.

The family never speaks of the incident, and Maya convinces herself that Mr. Freeman was killed because she lied in order to condemn him. Thinking that she has sold herself to the Devil, Maya resolves to protect others by not speaking to anyone except Bailey. At first the family accepts her silence as fallout from the rape, but after some time, they feel offended and become angry and violent with her.

SUMMARY: CHAPTER 14

Maya and Bailey return to Stamps, though Maya is not sure whether Momma has sent for them or whether her St. Louis family simple became unable to handle her silence. Bailey misses Vivian, but Maya finds herself relieved to return to the barren world of Stamps. Bailey exaggerates the wonders of the big city to the curious residents, developing his sarcastic tone, but no one notices his insults. He remains kind only to Maya. She understands Bailey's frustration, and he understands her silence.

SUMMARY: CHAPTER 15

Mrs. Bertha Flowers, whom Maya reveres as the "aristocrat of Black Stamps," plans to take Maya under her wing and prod her out of her silence. She invites Maya to her house and gives her some books and tells her to read them aloud. Maya delights to find that Mrs. Flowers has made cookies specifically for her. After reading, aloud and impressing Maya with her abilities, Mrs. Flowers assigns Maya the task of memorizing a poem to recite during her next visit. Maya returns exuberantly to the Store with the books and a bag of cookies for Bailey. Finally using her voice, Maya announces that Mrs. Flowers baked some cookies for Bailey. However, Momma flies into a rage and whips Maya because she used a phrase that Momma obscurely found offensive to God.

ANALYSIS: CHAPTERS 11–15

Whereas in previous chapters, Maya almost begins to appreciate and grow within her surroundings in St. Louis, her guilt-ridden response to Mr. Freeman's sexual molestation reveals that she has not adjusted well to her parental abandonment and life of isolation. Mr. Freeman takes advantage of Maya because she has never experienced much physical contact or affection, and she confuses Mr. Freeman's exploitative behavior with the physical attention she has yet to receive as a child. Maya's need for physical contact confuses the incident in her mind so much that she interprets Mr. Freeman's threat to kill Bailey as an indication that *she* has done something wrong, although she cannot say what.

Mr. Freeman also takes advantage of Maya's caring personality, especially her tendency to care for people in similar positions of neglect and pain. Perhaps trying to foreshadow the rape, Maya shows that she spent much time observing Mr. Freeman as he pathetically awaited Vivian's return in the evenings. Maya notes that Mr. Freeman has breasts like deflated female breasts and how she feels sorry for him. After the two separate incidences of sexual molestation, Mr. Freeman ignores Maya for weeks, augmenting her feelings of rejection and guilt.

Even though Maya further isolates herself in the library, the books do more good than harm. On the one hand, Maya's favorite stories and fairy-tales teach her the culturally accepted notion that women cannot be heroes, causing her to wish that she could be male. Nevertheless, Maya ceases to want or need Mr. Freeman's attention because books provide her with companionship. When Mr. Freeman rapes her, he uses the need for affection she previously expressed to blame her for his abuses. When she expresses reluctance to come anywhere near him, he accuses her of enjoying being near him before.

Maya highlights the idea that even though blacks suffer from racism and oppression, they remain individuals who can inflict suffering on other people. It is highly probable that some of the Baxter family's associates in the criminal underground—if not Maya's uncles themselves—killed Mr. Freeman. When the policeman casually reports that Mr. Freeman has been beaten to death, Grandmother Baxter tells the children never to mention Mr. Freeman's name or what they have heard about his death. Afterward, Maya's family viciously chastises her for being silent.

Even though many of the adults in Maya's life show their flaws, Maya continues to receive attention and care from others. The fact that Maya and Bailey have begun to grow naturally apart perhaps exacerbates Maya's isolation and confusion, but Bailey remains the most important person in her life. He persuades her to reveal the identity of the rapist, and his tearful reaction to learning that the man who lived with him raped Maya reveals the loving support he gives her. Bailey does not betray her trust. He never blames her for the rape or for their sudden return to Stamps. Once there, Mrs. Flowers offers Maya a way to speak without fear. Maya welcomes their return to Stamps because life there is predictable, but both Maya's silence and a general silence regarding the rape persist, and she continues to carry her unarticulated burden of guilt. Reading aloud from books or reciting poems with Mrs. Flowers allows Maya to speak through the words of others. Maya considers Mrs. Flowers a hero and thus shows that she has begun to forget, to a certain extent, the fact that books portray only males as heroes.

Maya's immediate reaction to having to lie in court and her subsequent self-imposed silence reveal her strong moral conscience. First, Maya shows that she hates that she must lie out of necessity in the courtroom. She says she now despises Mr. Freeman for causing her to tell a lie, indicating that she may even hate Mr. Freeman more for making her lie than for the rape itself. Moreover, despite the apparent fact that her vicious uncles, enabled by a loose and corrupt legal system, murder Mr. Freeman, Maya feels that her lie in court ultimately caused his death.

At the same time, Maya's attention to her own guilt concerning matters related to Mr. Freeman does not mean that she feels particularly guilty for the rape itself. Rather, she continues to refer to Mr. Freeman as a "dirty man," and she begins to strengthen her opinion of herself as an experienced woman. When she enters the courtroom filled with unsavory characters and "smirking mouths," Maya remembers that the nurses have told her that she has seen the worst life has to offer her, and she uses their words to bolster her confidence. She says, "I was eight, and grown," showing how the incident ultimately sharpens her precocious sense of self. Undoubtedly, she has lost some of the innocence that led to her accept Mr. Freeman's advances. Now, she puts the rape behind her to a certain extent and pays even more attention to her own character. Throughout the rest of the book, however, Maya must continue to struggle with growing pains, particularly those associated with sex. While she may grow wiser in some ways in St. Louis, she nevertheless remains a confused child.

CHAPTERS 16–19

SUMMARY: CHAPTER 16
Maya takes a job in Mrs. Viola Cullinan's home at the age of ten. The cook, Miss Glory, a descendant of the slaves once owned by the Cullinans, informs Maya that Mrs. Cullinan could not have children and Maya feels pity for Mrs. Cullinan. One day, one of Mrs. Cullinan's friends infuriates Maya when she suggests that Mrs. Cullinan call Maya "Mary" because "Margaret" is too long. Even worse, Maya notes, her name is Marguerite, not Margaret. When Mrs. Cullinan begins calling her Mary, Maya becomes furious. She knows Momma will not allow her to quit, so she decides she must find a way to get fired. She deliberately slacks in her work, but to no avail. Maya then takes Bailey's advice and breaks some of Mrs. Cullinan's heirloom china, making it look like an accident. Mrs. Cullinan drops her veneer of genteel racism and insults Maya with a racist slur. Upon hearing Mrs. Cullinan's sobs and screams, her friends crowd into the kitchen and one of them asks if "Mary" is responsible. Mrs. Cullinan screams, "Her name's Margaret."

SUMMARY: CHAPTER 17
One evening, Bailey stays out until well after dark. Willie and Momma do not mention their concern, but Momma takes Maya with her to search for Bailey. They find Bailey trudging home, but he does not offer an explanation for his lateness. He stoically receives a severe whipping, and Maya notes that for days it seems like Bailey has no soul. Later Bailey explains to Maya that he was late because he had seen a movie starring a white actress, Kay Francis, who looked like Vivian, and he stayed late to watch the movie a second time. They wait for weeks before another Kay Francis movie comes

to the theater. Maya laughs at the irony of a beloved white actress looking just like her black mother. The movie delights Maya, but it saddens Bailey. On the way home, he frightens Maya by dashing across the tracks in front of an oncoming railway car. Maya wonders if Bailey would ever jump on one of the trains and go away. A year later, he boards a boxcar, but succeeds only in stranding himself in Baton Rouge for two weeks.

SUMMARY: CHAPTER 18

The annual revival meeting interrupts the harsh daily existence in Stamps. People from all the black churches attend. This year, the preacher delivers a sermon admonishing those who practice false charity. Everyone knows it is a diatribe against white Christian hypocrisy. They give to poor blacks with the expectation that the recipient be humble and self-belittling in return. The sermon promises divine revenge and divine justice.

Afterward, the preacher announces that the unsaved should come forward and choose which church they want to join. Maya remarks that no minister has ever worked to gather members for different churches. She says he is practicing charity. Afterward, everyone relishes the sensation of righteousness. However, when they pass a noisy, secular, honky-tonk party, they fall silent and bow their heads, sensing again the presence of sin in the black world. Nevertheless, Maya notes that, to an outsider, those who attend the revival and those who visit the honky-tonk that night both appear to be trying to escape their harsh lives.

SUMMARY: CHAPTER 19

> My race groaned. It was our people falling. It was
> another lynching, yet another Black man hanging on a
> tree. . . . This might be the end of the world. If Joe lost
> we were back in slavery and beyond help.
> (See QUOTATIONS, p. 53)

People crowd inside the Store to listen to the heavyweight championship boxing match on the radio, desperately hoping that Joe Louis, a hero for the black community, will defend his title. Maya explains that if Louis were to lose, everything racist whites say about blacks would be true. His loss would represent and justify another lynching, another raped black woman, another beaten black boy. When Louis wins the fight, everyone in the Store celebrates with abandon. Maya says that Louis proves that blacks are the most powerful people in the world.

ANALYSIS: CHAPTERS 16–19

Maya's indignation toward Mrs. Cullinan for presumptuously renaming her attests to Maya's strong pride in her self, now revealed in the face of complex racist forces. Mrs. Cullinan does not bother to learn Maya's real name, Marguerite, and she chooses to change it for her own convenience. She does not exhibit violent racism, but she perpetrates an indignity that American blacks have faced throughout history. Mrs. Cullinan's renaming constitutes yet another form of displacement for Maya, this time racial displacement. She remarks upon the danger associated with calling a black person anything that could be loosely interpreted as insulting because blacks have been labeled negatively for centuries as "niggers, jigs, dinges, blackbirds, crows, boots and spooks." Maya's reaction to Mrs. Cullinan's re-naming exemplifies the subtle forms of resistance available to American blacks. Maya cannot directly demand recognition of her identity, but she finds a subversive form of resistance. This resistance powerfully affects Mrs. Cullinan. By switching back to Margaret, Mrs. Cullinan believes that she has reasserted her power over Maya as well as protected the holy name Mary from tarnish. Essentially, however, she has relinquished the name that was her symbol of power over Maya. Mary may have been under her control, but Margaret is not. Maya regains her name and her sense of self.

Maya describes numerous other instances of subtle black resistance to racism in these chapters. The black southern church is an avenue for subversive resistance. At the revival, the preacher gives a sermon that criticizes white power without directly naming it. His diatribe against greedy, self-righteous employers clearly attacks white farmers for paying miserable wages to black field labor. Movies and other popular culture of the 1930s disseminated terribly demeaning racial stereotypes of blacks. However, Maya's secret joke in the movie theater allows her a kind of resistance against the movie's negative portrayals of black people. Maya laughs in response to the Kay Francis movie because the white actress adored by the white audience looks like her mother, a black woman. Incidentally, at the same time that Maya delights in this irony, Bailey clearly suffers with longing for his mother. Just seeing her likeness sends him into a deep melancholy. The intensity of his feelings will eventually create a rift between him and Maya symbolized and fore-shadowed here by his running recklessly across the train tracks and abandoning Maya on the other side.

Despite recognizing the personally empowering nature of these instances of resistance, Maya's descriptions illustrate that such resistance rarely affects great change, even within the African-American community. Instead, such resistance often simply serves to save the black community from drowning in the desperation and despair that envelops them. Maya's description of the symbolic meaning behind the boxing match between Joe Louis and a white challenger attests to the pervasive nature of racism in 1930s America. For Maya and the members of her community, Joe Louis's victory is an empowering repudiation of the negative stereotypes heaped upon blacks. Underlying their joy, however, the desperate fact remains: Louis must bear the hopes and dreams of the entire black American community. White society prevented most forms of black advancement. Moreover, the few black Americans who did advance received little public attention for their achievements. When they did successfully garner public acclaim, role models and heroes such as Louis became figures that the black community relied upon for strength.

Unfortunately, Maya notes, sometimes those who practice subtle forms of resistance defeat themselves. The desperation in the Store during the fight attests to both the highs and the potential lows of the psychological resistance. Immediately after the revival meeting, the spiritually invigorated revivalists hear the people partying at a honky-tonk and bow their heads. Maya notes that the crushing realities of their daily struggles begin to replace their short-lived happiness. Both the sinners at the honky-tonk and the revival members share the same desire to shake off their troubles. However, the individual revival members only see the differences and suffer from despair. Rather than seeing the honky-tonk as another form of subtle empowerment, the church community sees it as a burden.

CHAPTERS 20–22

SUMMARY: CHAPTER 20
During the annual summer fish fry, women show off their baking and men fish in the nearby pond. Music and the noises of children's

games fill the air. Maya wanders into a secluded clearing to sit on a tree and stare at the sky. Louise Kendricks, a pretty girl of the same age, comes upon her. At first shy toward each other, they soon hold hands and spin around while looking at the sky. They become best friends and spend hours trying to learn the complicated "Tut" language because it is even more esoteric than pig latin.

While in the seventh grade, Maya receives a note from an eighth-grader, Tommy Valdon, asking her to be his valentine. She shows it to Louise, and Louise explains that valentines mean love. Maya says aloud, "Not ever again." She does not explain what she means to Louise. They tear the note into tiny pieces and throw it into the wind. The day before Valentine's Day, Maya's teacher calls the children by name and reads aloud cards sent to them from the eighth-grade class. Tommy sends another letter to Maya, stating that he saw Maya and her friend tear up his note, but he does not think she meant to hurt his feelings. He still considers her his valentine even if she does not answer his letter. He signs the note with his initials. When Maya decides to throw caution to the wind and flirt with him, Tommy's crush has already begun to wane.

SUMMARY: CHAPTER 21

Bailey constructs a tent in the yard and begins playing sexual games with girls. Bailey plays the father, the girl plays the mother, and Maya plays the baby, sitting outside to stand guard. After six months, Bailey loses his virginity to Joyce, an older, well-developed girl. Bailey begins stealing things from the Store for her. After a few months, she disappears. Her aunt later tells Momma that Joyce ran away with a railroad porter whom she met at the Store. Momma becomes flustered thinking that something upsetting like that occurred under her nose. Bailey is heartbroken. Maya never liked Joyce, but she hates her for leaving and hurting Bailey. When Joyce was around, Maya notes, Bailey did not use sarcasm.

SUMMARY: CHAPTER 22

One stormy night, a fellow townsman named George Taylor comes to the Store and stays the night, still heartbroken over the death of his wife, Florida. Momma urges Mr. Taylor to be thankful for the forty years he spent with Florida, although, Momma says, it was a pity they never had children. At the mention of children, Mr. Taylor replies that Florida appeared before him the night before and told him that she wanted children. Momma and Willie ask if he had been dreaming of Florida, but Mr. Taylor insists that he was awake. Maya has always hated the custom of telling ghost stories, but Mr. Taylor's account scares her even more because he insists it is real.

To occupy herself otherwise, Maya remembers that she went to Florida's funeral. She did not want to go, but Florida had left her yellow brooch to Maya, and Momma insisted that she attend the services. The experience turned out to be Maya's first confrontation with mortality. At the funeral, Florida seemed to her like the short-lived mud sculptures so often made by children playing in the summer.

Returning from her memory, Maya cannot help but hear Mr. Taylor narrating his experience. The night before, he saw a fat, blond, blue-eyed baby angel laughing at him. He heard his wife's moaning voice, and the angel laughed harder. Eventually, Mrs. Taylor's voice moaned that she wanted children.

Momma suggests that if it was not a dream, maybe Mrs. Taylor wants him to work with the children in the church. The atmosphere of eerie gloom passes when the conversation returns to mundane, everyday things. Maya climbs into bed with Momma, secure in the knowledge that she could drive away scary spirits.

ANALYSIS: CHAPTERS 20–22

Louise's friendship provides Maya with her first opportunity to enjoy her youth and, to a certain extent, her independence. Maya's experiences prior to their friendship have matured her beyond her years, and Louise is her first childhood friend. Before, Maya moved and interacted largely in a world of adults, with the exception of Bailey. With Louise, Maya begins to experience being a young girl for the first time, playing games, inventing languages, discussing boys and young love. It is also Maya's first relationship that occurs outside her family and apart from her family's influence. Whereas Momma may have arranged for Mrs. Flowers to show Maya attention, here Maya meets her friend while trying to find a private place to relieve herself in the forest. As they spin each other around and look up at the sky, their meeting takes on a magical quality, suggesting its importance in Maya's development as an individual.

Although Tommy Valdon and the valentine's crush never leads to romance, it restores some of the innocence in Maya that Mr. Freeman stole from her. In part, Maya feels threatened by the valentine because she has no experience with adolescent crushes. Mainly, however, the rape and its aftermath have led her to distrust anything having to do with both sexual and romantic love. Maya clearly announces that she will not let another man or boy treat her as Mr. Freeman did. Tommy's second letter, however, states that his affection will not change even if Maya chooses not to respond. Hearing this, Maya feels more secure because Tommy obviously feels genuine affection for Maya and her personality. Unlike Mr. Freeman, the valentine does not represent any physical expectation from Maya, and, sensing his good intentions, she begins to flirt shyly and innocently with him.

Although less malicious, Joyce's power over Bailey parallels Mr. Freeman's power over Maya. Joyce takes advantage of Bailey's frustrated love for his mother in the same way that Mr. Freeman's advances prey on Maya's frustrated need for physical affection. Looking back on the relationship, Maya remarks that Joyce—who is four years older than Bailey—represents for Bailey the mother who let him get close to her and the sister who was never withdrawn. To a certain extent, moreover, Joyce takes advantage of Bailey as well. As long as Bailey provides her with stolen spoils from the Store, Joyce gives him the affection he craves. She turns Bailey's innocent, curious games into sexual intercourse, taking his virginity, and then leaves him in the dust. Maya notes that Joyce has a positive effect on Bailey while she is around, but when Joyce skips town, Bailey reveals not just his displeasure at the fact that she has left but also his sense that the situation was not ideal in the first place. When Maya asks him about Joyce, Bailey feigns disinterest at first, but then he says that Joyce has chosen someone who will give her sex all the time, perhaps indicating his understanding that he and Joyce used their relationship for different purposes.

In light of Mr. Taylor's ghost story, it is important to note that storytelling and imagination, accounts of spirits, the conjuring of images and beings from the past, and even superstition all played vital roles in the African-American tradition. Just as the Christian church provided slaves, former slaves, and their descendants with a sense of salvation and hope, storytelling and folklore provided them with a form of not just entertainment but empowerment. Because white colonists and Americans drastically altered the lives of slaves and essentially erased their connection with their homeland and their past, slaves began writing their own history through storytelling. (For more information, see Suggestions for Further Reading.) In this case, Mr. Taylor's ghost story reveals the pervasive nature of

SUMMARY & ANALYSIS

tense race relations and conjures up the frightening baby angel as being blond-haired and blue-eyed. Momma's dialogue with Mr. Taylor steers the conversation to everyday things and dispels the eerie gloom that the ghost story cast over the room. Momma has, in her way, cast out the specters of malevolent spirits with her quiet determined attention to the details of everyday living.

CHAPTERS 23–26

SUMMARY: CHAPTER 23

Maya notes that black families in Stamps consider the eighth-grade graduation a great event. When Maya takes her seat in the school auditorium, however, she feels uneasy. The white speaker, Mr. Edward Donleavy, gives a speech about the improvements in the local schools. The white school has received new lab equipment for science classes thanks to his efforts. He also states that he has bragged to many important people that several great college athletes graduated from Maya's school. Maya feels that he has blemished the joy of the graduation day by insinuating that black children only achieved greatness through sports, not through academics. The members of the eighth-grade class hang their heads in shame. Maya laments the fact that she has no control over her life and wishes that Christopher Columbus never sailed to the New World. After his speech, Donleavy rushes to leave.

Henry Reed's valedictory speech dispels the dismal atmosphere, but Maya reacts with cynicism and pessimism. Henry continues to speak with strength and clarity, and afterward he turns his back to the audience and addresses the graduating class sitting on the stage. He leads them in "Lift Ev'ry Voice and Sing," a song known popularly as the Negro National Anthem. Maya listens to the words for the very first time, drops her cynical attitude, and takes pride in her black community.

SUMMARY: CHAPTER 24

Maya develops an excruciating toothache. The nearest black dentist practices twenty-five miles away, so Momma takes Maya to see Dr. Lincoln, a white dentist in town. During the Great Depression, Momma loaned money to many people, including Dr. Lincoln. Now she believes he owes her a favor. When they arrive, Dr. Lincoln states that he does not treat black patients. Momma reminds him that her generous loan saved him before. He reminds her that he repaid the loan, adding that he would rather stick his hand in a dog's mouth than in Maya's black mouth. Momma leaves Maya outside and advances into Dr. Lincoln's office. Maya imagines Momma as a superhero, wielding her powers and forbidding Dr. Lincoln ever to work in Stamps again. In reality, Momma tells Dr. Lincoln that he owes her interest on the loan she previously made to him. He protests, saying that she never asked for interest before, but he pays her the ten dollars, demanding a receipt to seal the deal. Afterward, Momma takes Maya to the black dentist in Texarkana. Talking with Uncle Willie later on, Momma indicates that even though she sinned in making Dr. Lincoln pay interest retroactively, he deserved it.

SUMMARY: CHAPTER 25

> He was away in a mystery, locked in the enigma that
> young Southern Black boys start to unravel, start to
> try to unravel, from seven years old to death.
>
> (See QUOTATIONS, p. 54)

One day, Bailey returns home from an errand, pale and shaken. He asks what black people did to white people to incite so much hatred. He has just seen a black man's dead, rotting body pulled from a pond. Grinning at the body, a white man ordered Bailey to help load the man into the wagon and then pretended that he was going to lock Bailey and the other black men in with the dead body. Not long afterward, Momma begins planning a trip to take Bailey and Maya to live in California with their mother.

SUMMARY: CHAPTER 26

Momma lives in Los Angeles with Bailey and Maya while Vivian makes living arrangements for her children. Maya and Bailey begin to see Vivian not just as a superhuman beauty but also as a real person with fears and insecurities of her own. Vivian seems concerned with her children's well-being and even throws them a special party one night at two-thirty in the morning, enchanting Maya with her fun-loving and spontaneous nature.

Although trained as a nurse, Vivian supports herself and her children by running poker games or gambling. Maya notes that even though Vivian exhibits temperamental, melodramatic outbursts, she never compromises fairness. Maya discusses Vivian's power and her honesty. Once, Maya recalls, Vivian shot one of her partners for verbally insulting her, and afterward, they retained their mutual admiration for each other. After all, Vivian had warned him that she would shoot before pulling the trigger.

Soon after, the U.S. enters World War II and Vivian marries Daddy Clidell, a successful businessman. The family moves to San Francisco.

ANALYSIS: 23–26

Edward Donleavy's speech is a slap in the black community's face. The black community's excitement over the graduation comes from the fact that they have had to fight very hard to receive even a modicum of education. Black activists of earlier generations had fought to build schools for black children. Before emancipation, educational opportunities for African-Americans were rare, especially in the South. After emancipation, black Americans faced hostility toward their education from their former masters. In Stamps, the graduating eighth-grade and high-school classes surmount the pressures of poverty and racism to earn their diplomas. Donleavy's speech indicates that their achievements in education are worthless and misdirected. The white school has received tangible improvements aimed at increasing and bettering the opportunities for white students in science and art, but Donleavy's description of bragging about the college athletes from their school suggests, at best, that the black schools do not receive tangible improvements like the science equipment and new art teacher at the white school. Unfortunately, Donleavy's remarks shame the black children into bowing their heads and thinking that they should not value their education and their graduation. Maya remarks that Donleavy "exposed" them. Even more insulting, Donleavy expects the students and their parents to be grateful to him for his pathetic efforts.

Momma's confrontation with Dr. Lincoln introduces the important idea of the ethics of necessity in Maya's autobiography. Maya imagines that Momma battles Dr. Lincoln and brings him to his knees, but in reality Momma compromises her own sense of ethics in order to extract money from Dr. Lincoln. Momma admits that it is wrong to demand interest on a loan retroactively. To a certain extent, Maya's dire situation spurred Momma to demand the interest. The ethics of necessity, however, applies more to the fact that Momma wants Dr. Lincoln to pay for his evil, racist refusal to treat Maya, and for his ingratitude toward the humane and generous black woman (Momma) who saved his practice with her money. Momma does not really consider her compromise to be a bad thing, for she and Willie laugh about the incident while discussing it. The ethics of necessity by which blacks justify lying or even illegal actions to achieve retribution toward whites continues to operate in the autobiography, particularly in San Francisco, when Maya meets Daddy Clidell's con-artist friends. It differs greatly, however, from the type of serious criminal activity exhibited by Maya's family in St. Louis.

Momma's decision to take Bailey and Maya to California exemplifies her practical nature as well. This time, however, Momma does not laugh while making this sacrifice. In this case, she shows her quiet bravery. She loves her grandchildren so much that she decides to part with them. She chooses to save them from further ugly encounters with racist Southern whites. Although she has never before traveled more than fifty miles from her place of birth, Momma leaves Willie and her business to live in Los Angeles for six months while her grandchildren settle into their new life. The calm with which she makes the abrupt change shows a steely, resourceful character.

Maya's reversal from disgust to pride during the graduation shows that she has begun to take serious pride in being a member of a resilient black community. Donleavy's speech makes Maya terribly angry, to the point where she imagines a retelling of history that is just as murderous and violent toward white people as toward blacks. Not even Henry Reed's beautiful speech can pull Maya out of her pessimism. However, when Henry invokes the Negro National Anthem, he reminds the audience, his fellow graduates, and eventually Maya that they should retain their pride in themselves and their abilities. Maya comes to realize that other black people have worked hard to provide her with the opportunity to graduate from school. Perhaps more important to Maya's development, given her love for literature and poetry, she comes to understand that blacks have written poetry and literature in celebration of black identity and achievement. Maya remarks that, before, she paid attention only to Patrick Henry and other white freedom fighters. Now, she listens for the first time to the words of James Weldon Johnson's inspirational song "Lift Ev'ry Voice and Sing" and no longer considers herself just a member of the graduating class, but also a member of "the wonderful, beautiful Negro race." As an adult looking back, Maya thanks black artists and poets for helping her to sustain her hope and realize her black pride in the midst of disappointment and discouragement.

CHAPTERS 27–31

SUMMARY: CHAPTERS 27 & 28

Maya comments on the changes that occur in San Francisco after the U.S. enters World War II. Provincial black migrants, not dissimilar to the people Maya knew in Stamps, flow into the city, working side by side with illiterate whites in the defense industry. The black workers replace the Japanese, who have been unjustly interned by the U.S. government in camps. Maya notes that no one ever speaks about the Japanese displacement. She says the black community unconsciously pays little attention to the Japanese because blacks focus on advancing themselves in the face of white prejudice.

The constant aura of change and displacement in wartime San Francisco makes Maya feel at home for the first time in her life. Upon her entrance into school, she automatically gets promoted a grade and later transfers to a white school where she is one of only three black students. The white students appear aggressive and better educated. Maya remembers only one teacher from school, Miss Kirwin, who never played favorites and never treated Maya differently for being black. When she is fourteen, Maya receives a scholarship to the California Labor School where she studies dance and drama.

SUMMARY: CHAPTER 29

The owner of numerous apartment buildings and pool halls, Daddy Clidell becomes the only true father figure Maya ever knows. She loves his strength and his tenderness. He is dignified, but not haughty. He has no inferiority complex about receiving little education, but he also lacks the arrogance usually associated with men of great accomplishment. Daddy Clidell introduces Maya to his con-men friends who have learned to swindle bigoted whites. They once conned a racist white man from Tulsa who had a history of cheating blacks into paying $40,000 for a piece of property that did not exist. Maya cannot regard the con men as criminals because she says the deck has been stacked against them from the start anyway. Ethics, she notes, depends upon necessity and are therefore different in the black community.

SUMMARY: CHAPTER 30

Big Bailey invites Maya to spend the summer with him and his girl-friend, Dolores. Dolores and Maya exchange letters and anticipate incorrectly each other's physical appearance. Both Dolores and Maya are shocked when they meet for the first time. Big Bailey has promised to marry Dolores, but he keeps postponing the wedding plans. Much to Maya's surprise, they live in a low-class mobile home. Nevertheless, Dolores tries to maintain the home in prim-and-proper style, and Maya's messy nature disturbs Dolores from the beginning. Big Bailey watches the mutual discomfort between Maya and Dolores with amusement.

A fluent speaker of Spanish and an avid chef both by trade and in the home, Big Bailey makes frequent trips to Mexico supposedly to buy groceries. One day Big Bailey invites Maya on one of his shop-ping trips, inciting Dolores's jealousy. During the trip, he jokes with a guard by offering Maya to him as a wife. He drives past the border towns and stops outside Ensenada. Women, men, and children greet him warmly. Big Bailey becomes a different person. He relaxes and stops putting on airs. Maya, who knows a bit of Spanish from school, begins to enjoy herself, but when she cannot find her father later in the evening, she becomes frightened and sits alone in the car, waiting for him. Eventually he staggers out drunk and passes out in the car. Maya drives fifty miles back to the border even though she has never driven a car before, let alone one with a clutch. She has a minor acci-dent at the checkpoint. Big Bailey regains consciousness and settles the matter before driving the rest of the way home. He is neither sur-prised nor angry about the accident. He does not seem surprised that Maya could drive, and Maya dislikes the fact that he does not appre-ciate the magnitude of her achievement. They ride home in silence.

SUMMARY: CHAPTER 31

After returning home, Maya overhears an argument between Dolores and Big Bailey. Dolores feels that Maya has come between them. Big Bailey leaves the house in a huff, leaving Dolores sob-bing alone. Maya approaches Dolores and tells her that she never meant to come between them. Maya feels strong and honorable doing her good deed, but Dolores rebuffs Maya's peaceful gesture and insults her, calling her mother, Vivian, a whore. Furious, Maya tells Dolores she is going to slap her and then does so. Dolores retaliates and Maya realizes that Dolores has stabbed her with scis-sors. Bleeding, Maya runs out of the house and locks herself in her father's car. Big Bailey hears Dolores screaming and returns to investigate. He takes Dolores inside the house then drives Maya, who feels empowered by the events, to a friend's house, where a woman bandages Maya's wound. Afterward, he drives her to the home of another friend, where she spends the night. Big Bailey visits her at noon the next day and gives her some money, promising to return later that evening. Dreading having to face her father's friends, Maya packs some food and leaves. She cannot return to Vivian, however, because she would never be able to hide her wound. Telling Vivian would only precipitate trouble between Vivian and Big Bailey, and Maya guiltily remembers Mr. Freeman's death all too clearly.

ANALYSIS: CHAPTERS 27–31

San Francisco represents an entirely different world from the rural South. Maya attends an unsegregated school. Her education becomes more varied with the addition of drama and dance to her studies. As opposed to the monotony of life in the South, San Francisco undergoes constant change, especially due to the upheaval of the war. Similar to the Great Migration in the East, the defense industry's factories went into full swing in California during the war, and they employed willing blacks and whites alike, especially since the Japanese population had been moved unjustly to internment camps. This harrowing scene of constant displacement becomes, somewhat ironically, the first place where Maya feels a sense of belonging, giving her a new boldness and an awareness of herself. Maya has never felt that she belongs anywhere before, and the constant scene of changing faces in wartime San Francisco—the cyclical wave of newcomers—wards off her own sense of alienation and isolation.

Maya's descriptions of a multiracial apartment building and an unsegregated school might lead one to think that racial relations were not as tense as they were in the South, but she takes care to explain that this was not the case. The outer face of San Francisco did not show the tumult within. Rural whites brought their prejudices with them to the city. Rural blacks came to the city with their distrust of white people, cultivated through years of negative experiences. In the South, blacks and poor whites lived and worked on unequal, opposite sides of the racial divide. In San Francisco, they worked side by side in the war industry.

In San Francisco, Maya encounters a more brash form of resistance to racial inequality. Whereas Momma thought it sinful yet necessary to insist that Dr. Lincoln pay ten dollars in interest when she had not asked for it initially, Daddy Clidell's friends lie and cheat to make $40,000 off white men. Momma's quiet rebellions were replaced by the financially rewarding methods of Daddy Clidell's friends, who catered to racial stereotypes in order to lure racist whites into their con games. They learned to turn white prejudice into a liability for whites. Despite the difference between Momma and the con-men's methods, Maya shows that in both cases the ethical standard is based on necessity and justifies the means used to produce change. The standard of ethics differs for the black community because if people cannot compete equally in society, they must find ways to advance by manipulating the system. Fair play ceased to have moral value when the rules of the game proved unfair. For the most part, the cotton-field laborers in Stamps accepted their difficult existence with resignation. Their resistance came in the form of personal empowerment and psychological stamina. The wartime generation, however, gained a sense of entitlement and wielded its creative powers to act upon it.

Nearly every scene in these chapters illustrates Maya's blossoming awareness of, and her love and respect for, herself. Maya's emboldened sense of self shines forth in her impulsive decision to drive the car back to the U.S. from Mexico. Even though she has an accident, she says that she felt better than at any other time in her life. Maya is so confident in herself and proud of her achievement that she declares that she did not even need her father's praise at first, even though she becomes angry when he continues to ignore her accomplishment. When Big Bailey asks Maya about her opinion of Dolores, Maya remarks upon Dolores's pettiness and says that Dolores does not like her based upon her physical appearance. After overhearing the argument between Big Bailey and Dolores, Maya feels heroic and merciful when she tries to console Dolores. Maya has changed from a self-conscious and nervous girl to a defiant young woman, perhaps remaking herself in the image of the strong women who have influenced her. Indeed, besides the obvious parallels to Momma's dignified nature, Maya acts very much like Vivian, particularly when she warns Dolores before slapping her in the same way that Vivian warned her partner before shooting him.

In these chapters, Maya compares Big Bailey's lack of paternal graces with Daddy Clidell's strength as a father figure. Maya's description of Big Bailey's reaction to the confrontation and the injury hints at sarcasm and shows that she considers Big Bailey to be utterly selfish, even if he comes across as a likable character. He chooses to take Maya to a friend for treatment of her wound instead of a doctor because he wants to avoid personal embarrassment. He does not directly ask Maya to keep quiet about the incident, but he implies that she should do so, explaining how a scandal could damage his reputation. As if speaking for Big Bailey but with a melodramatic flare, Maya asks the reader rhetorically, "Could I imagine the scandal if people found out that his, Bailey Johnson's, daughter had been cut by his lady friend?" She ironically exaggerates the response to her question by saying that all black people in the city would hang their heads in shame if Big Bailey's troubles became known publicly. Daddy Clidell, on the other hand, shows his pride when people think that Maya is his biological daughter. He has no insecurities to hide and no superiority to flaunt. As a result, he gives Maya affection and respect, and she considers him the first real father figure in her life.

CHAPTERS 32–36

SUMMARY: CHAPTER 32
After leaving Big Bailey's friends' house, Maya spends the night in a car in a junkyard. When she wakes, a group of black, Mexican, and white homeless teenagers stand outside laughing at her through the windows. They tell her she can stay as long as she follows the rules: people of the opposite sex cannot sleep together, stealing is forbidden because it attracts police attention, and everyone works, committing their earnings to the community. Maya stays for a month. Everyone enters a dance contest on Saturday nights, and Maya and her partner win second prize during her last weekend. Maya learns to appreciate diversity and tolerance fully that month, something that influences her the rest of her life, she notes in retrospect. At the end of the summer, Maya calls Vivian and asks her to pay her airfare to San Francisco. The group accepts the news of her impending departure with detachment, although everyone wishes her well.

SUMMARY: CHAPTER 33
Maya notes that she has changed much since the start of the summer, but Bailey, who also seems to have aged significantly, shows indifference toward Maya's tales. Still, they share an interest in

dancing and become a sensation at the big-band dances in the city auditorium. Meanwhile, Maya notes, Bailey and Vivian have become estranged. Unconsciously seeking Vivian's approval, Bailey begins wearing flashy clothing and dating a white prostitute, trying to model himself after Vivian's male associates. Vivian seems unaware that her own preferences have influenced his tastes. She demands that he stop dating the white prostitute, and he begins disobeying her rules. Eventually, Bailey moves out. He and Vivian quickly reconcile, and she promises to arrange a job for him in the South Pacific. Meanwhile, Maya acts as a neutral party but becomes terribly upset when Bailey moves out. Bailey assures her that he has a mature mind and that the time has come for him to leave the nest.

SUMMARY: CHAPTER 34

> *The Black female is assaulted in her tender years by all those common forces of nature at the same time that she is caught in the tripartite crossfire of masculine prejudice, white illogical hate and Black lack of power.* (See QUOTATIONS, p. 55)

Maya decides to take a semester off from school and work. For weeks, she persists in trying to get a job as a streetcar conductor despite racist hiring policies. She finally succeeds in becoming the first black person to work on the San Francisco streetcars. When she returns to school, she feels out of place among her classmates. American black women, she says, must not only face the common problems associated with adolescence, but also racism and sexism. Therefore, it does not surprise her that black women who survive these conflicts possess strong characters.

SUMMARY: CHAPTER 35

The Well of Loneliness (a classic work of 1920s lesbian fiction by Radclyffe Hall) is Maya's first introduction to lesbianism. She does not really understand what a lesbian is, and she begins to fear that she is turning into one because she confuses lesbianism with being a hermaphrodite. She notes that she has a deep voice, underdeveloped breasts and hips, and no under-arm hair. She resolves to ask Vivian about a strange growth on her vagina. Vivian explains that the changes are perfectly normal.

Vivian's answer relieves Maya, but she still has unanswered fears about whether she might be a lesbian. Maya decides to get a boyfriend to settle the matter once and for all. However, all of her male acquaintances busily chase light-skinned, straight-haired girls. Maya casually and frankly propositions one of two handsome brothers who live near her, but their unromantic, unsatisfying encounter does not relieve her anxieties about being an abnormal girl. Three weeks later, she discovers that she is pregnant.

SUMMARY: CHAPTER 36

Maya accepts full responsibility for her pregnancy. She writes to Bailey for advice, and he tells her to keep it a secret. Vivian opposes abortions, and he fears she would make Maya quit school. Maya throws herself into school and confesses after graduating that she is eight months pregnant. Vivian and Daddy Clidell calmly accept Maya's impending, unwed motherhood without condemnation.

Maya gives birth to a son. She is fascinated by the baby and afraid to touch him. Vivian finally makes Maya sleep with her three-week-old son. Fearing that she will crush him, Maya attempts unsuccessfully to stay awake all night. Vivian wakes her later to show how the baby lies, resting comfortably in the crook of her arm. Vivian tells Maya that she does not have to worry about doing the right thing because if her heart is in the right place, she will do the right thing regardless. Maya peacefully returns to sleep next to her son.

ANALYSIS: CHAPTERS 32–36

The final chapters of *I Know Why the Caged Bird Sings* detail Maya's rapid journey into adulthood. Maya experiences important intellectual growth while staying in the junkyard. After a month, she says, "[M]y thinking processes had so changed that I was hardly recognizable to myself." Before she stays in the junkyard, she has limited contact with people of other races. That month in the junkyard, she forms full-fledged friendships with Mexican and white teenagers. Her acceptance into such a mixed group proves an unusual experience, considering her isolated childhood. She feels that she is part of the greater human race.

The experience in the junkyard also shows that Maya's growing sense of independence and confidence in her self has begun to coalesce and intensify. Only days before, she surprised herself by driving the car in Mexico, and now she strikes out on her own to spend a month in a junkyard living in a responsibly managed communal society. The intensity of her poise and self-assurance fuels her quest for the position on the streetcar when she returns home to San Francisco. Other employers desperately seek laborers at higher wages without discrimination, yet Maya refuses to give up the job she has chosen. At age fifteen, she has developed a surprising adult will. Once hired, she ceases to live in a world demarcated by black neighborhoods and continues to rush headlong into the larger world.

Nevertheless, Maya's most rapid affirmation of her induction into the world of adulthood—the birth of her baby boy—also symbolizes the fact that Maya is still a child in many ways. The final chapter details Maya's sensual awakening, not unlike the awakening of a typical adolescent, complete with fears and questions about sex and appearance. Angelou specifically references her youthful innocence when she uses the phrase "had I been older" in describing the incident with her classmate's beautiful breasts.

Just as Maya's rape appeared to be a direct result of her displacement, in some ways Maya's pregnancy results from her continued displacement from her mother Vivian. Vivian certainly takes Maya seriously when Maya questions her about sex. Vivian does not, however, take an active interest in finding out whether she has answered all of Maya's questions, thinking that everything will be all right once Maya washes her face, has a glass of milk, and returns to sleep. Even up until the end of the book, Vivian continues to look at Maya not out of the corner of her eye, but "out of the corner of her existence." Maya remains a child sexually and thus without parental guidance in matters concerning sex she is loosed to the world of sex and pregnancy and physical adulthood with only her own instincts to guide her.

The autobiography ends, however, with an overwhelmingly positive picture of Vivian. Vivian makes mistakes along the way, but she nevertheless survives with the strength and honesty that provide sustenance for and rub off on Maya in the end. When Maya becomes pregnant, Vivian supports and encourages her without condemnation, and she gives Maya her first and most important lesson about trusting her maternal instincts. Maya admires her unflinching honesty, her strength, and her caring nature, despite her frequent fumbling as a parent.

Angelou places both Vivian and even herself within the tradition of black women with strong characters and honorable survival mechanisms. Angelou says she often hears people react to the

formidable character of black women in America as if they are surprised or offended. This, in turn, surprises Angelou. She feels that
black women must struggle so much to survive that, when they do,
their formidable character is predictable. She goes on to say that
this inevitable strength of character should be respected if not
accepted with enthusiasm. Maya demonstrates that the universal
struggles of adolescence combine with the stresses of race and gender to make black women's struggles all the more challenging.

Even if one is unacquainted with Angelou's poem of the same
name, the title of *I Know Why the Caged Bird Sings* seems particularly apt given the subject matter of the book. Maya compares herself, her black female role models, and even her entire race to the
bird who is locked in a cage but nevertheless sings. Maya implies
that by reading her autobiography, the reader will come to understand why the bird sings despite being locked up in a cage. At the
same time, the title implies the possibility that the reason why the
caged bird sings could be a secret, one that Maya holds close inside
her, away from the tampering, meddling forces of the prison master.
We can guess why the bird sings—perhaps to break free, perhaps to
provide solace to itself, perhaps because its voice is its only means of
action or communication, or perhaps because the bird feels joy
knowing something others do not. Maya's widely varied and
insightful depiction of the African-American struggle affords many
possible reasons.

IMPORTANT QUOTATIONS EXPLAINED

1. If growing up is painful for the Southern Black
   girl, being aware of her displacement is the rust on
   the razor that threatens the throat. It is an
   unnecessary insult.

This vivid assertion ends the opening section of *I Know Why the Caged Bird Sings*. Although this section, which acts as a prologue, mostly emphasizes the point of view of Maya at five or six years old, this statement clearly comes from Angelou's adult voice. Looking back on her childhood experiences, Maya notes that she not only fell victim to a hostile, racist, and sexist society, but to other social forces as well, including the displacement she felt from her family and her peers. Maya feels displaced primarily because when she was three years old, her parents sent her away to live with her grandmother. This early separation, as well as subsequent ones, leaves her feeling rootless for most of her childhood. Angelou's autobiography likens the experience of growing up as a black girl in the segregated American South to having a razor at one's throat. Her constant awareness of her own displacement—the fact that she differed from other children in appearance and that she did not have a sense of belonging associated with anyone or anyplace—becomes the "unnecessary insult" that she must deal with at such a young age. Over the course of the work, Maya details numerous negative effects of such displacement, including her susceptibility to Mr. Freeman's sexual molestation.

2. A light shade had been pulled down between the Black community and all things white, but one could see through it enough to develop a fear-admiration-contempt for the white "things"—white folks' cars and white glistening houses and their children and their women. But above all, their wealth that allowed them to waste was the most enviable.

In this passage in Chapter 8, Angelou captures Maya's childlike observations about what makes white people different. Her fixation on clothing as a sign of difference also refers back to the incident in church when she suddenly realizes that her fairy-tale taffeta dress is really an old, faded white woman's hand-me-down. Stamps, Arkansas, suffers so thoroughly from segregation and Maya's world is so completely enmeshed in the black community that she often finds it hard to imagine what white people look like. They appear to her more like spectral ghosts with mysterious powers—and wonderful possessions—than as fellow human beings. At the same time, from a young age Maya knows that white people bear responsibility for the suffering of the cotton-pickers. She also learns from Momma that it is best not to address any white people directly, as it might lead to mortal danger. Momma goes so far as never to even speak about white people without using the title "they."

3.   My race groaned. It was our people falling. It was
     another lynching, yet another Black man hanging on a
     tree. One more woman ambushed and raped. . . . This
     might be the end of the world. If Joe lost we were back
     in slavery and beyond help. It would all be true, the
     accusations that we were lower types of human
     beings. Only a little higher than the apes.

In this scene in Chapter 19, Maya crowds around the Store's radio
with the rest of the community to listen to Joe Louis defend his
world heavyweight boxing title. As Maya conveys in this passage,
the entire black community has its hopes and psychological salvation bound up in the fists of Louis, "the Brown Bomber." This passage describes the precarious nature of black pride in the face of
hostile oppression, highlighting the staggering and wrenching significance this boxing match held for the community as the community teeters between salvation and despair. The rarity of black
people achieving public acclaim in both the black and white communities meant that the few who managed to do so had to bear the
expectations of the black community. The match becomes an
explicit staging of black against white. Louis's loss would mean the
"fall" of the race and a return to the idea that whites had a right to
denigrate black people. Cynics might say that Louis's win does little more than stave off the black community's psychological
despair. It does not turn the tables on whites because there is no
denying that whites still hold all the power. His public victory,
however, proves to blacks in the Store that they are the most powerful people in the world and enables them to live another day with
strength and vigor in the face of oppression. Racism plays many
psychological games with blacks and whites, and perhaps Louis's
public recognition helps to teach both whites and blacks to accept
African-Americans as equals.

QUOTATIONS

4. Bailey was talking so fast he forgot to stutter, he forgot to scratch his head and clean his fingernails with his teeth. He was away in a mystery, locked in the enigma that young Southern Black boys start to unravel, start to *try* to unravel, from seven years old to death. The humorless puzzle of inequality and hate.

In this passage in Chapter 25, Bailey reels from having encountered a dead, rotting black man and having witnessed a white man's light-hearted satisfaction at seeing the body. Maya emphasizes that the traumatic experience forces him to *try* to confront a degree of hatred that he cannot comprehend. Maya does not say that he succeeds in comprehending the reasoning behind white hatred. Bailey asks Uncle Willy to explain how colored people had offended whites originally, but both Uncle Willy and Momma try to hide the sickening, debilitating truth from Bailey. This section draws attention to the idea that Bailey's life depended upon him not understanding or attempting to understand how racism operates against black men. Bailey's experience here precipitates Momma's decision to remove the children from both the physical and psychological dangers associated with growing up in the South. This quote also illustrates the fact that while Angelou writes mostly about the experiences of black girls and women living in the segregated South, she also empathizes with the experiences of her male relatives.

5. The Black female is assaulted in her tender years by all those common forces of nature at the same time that she is caught in the tripartite crossfire of masculine prejudice, white illogical hate and Black lack of power. The fact that the adult American Negro female emerges a formidable character is often met with amazement, distaste and even belligerence.

This passage in Chapter 34 addresses why black women have strength of character. Maya says that most of the strong black women in her novel are "survivors." They have strong characters quite simply because they have survived against impossible odds. Therefore, they obviously show heroism, courage, and strength. Moreover, Maya states that the odds pitted against black women include not only the triple threat of sexism, racism, and black powerlessness, but also the simultaneous presence of "common forces of nature" that assault and confuse all children. Maya has had to grow up more quickly than the children around her. Her experiences—driving the car in Mexico, living in the junkyard, returning to witness Bailey move out of the house, and then successfully fighting to get a job as the first black conductor on the San Francisco streetcars, rather than go back to a school where she would not belong—have made her feel displaced and older than her years. Maya is already on her way toward becoming "a formidable character" as a result of the many assaults she deals with in "her tender years," but this does not mean that Maya is an adult. Maya's discussion of the "common forces of nature" foreshadows how her journey of survival has yet to meet the obstacles of adolescence, sexuality, and teenage pregnancy. These obstacles face all children, but for black females, they exacerbate an already difficult situation.

KEY FACTS

FULL TITLE
I Know Why the Caged Bird Sings

AUTHOR
Maya Angelou

TYPE OF WORK
Autobiographical novel

GENRE
Autobiography

LANGUAGE
English

TIME AND PLACE WRITTEN
New York City, late 1960s

DATE OF FIRST PUBLICATION
1969

PUBLISHER
Random House

NARRATOR
Maya Angelou

POINT OF VIEW
Maya Angelou speaks in the first person as she recounts her childhood. She writes both from a child's point of view and from her perspective as an adult.

TONE
Personal, comical, woeful, and philosophical

TENSE
Past

SETTING (TIME)
1930s–1950s

SETTING (PLACE)
Stamps, Arkansas; St. Louis, Missouri; Oakland, California; San Francisco, California

PROTAGONIST
Maya Angelou

MAJOR CONFLICT
Coming-of-age as a southern black girl, confronting racism, sexism, violence, and loneliness

RISING ACTION
Maya's parents divorce; Maya and Bailey are sent to Stamps; Maya and Bailey move in with their mother in St. Louis; Maya is raped; Maya and Bailey return to Stamps; Bailey witnesses a victim of lynching; Maya and Bailey move to San Francisco to live with Vivian; Maya spends the summer with her father

CLIMAX
Maya runs away from her father, displaying her first true act of self-reliance and independence after a lifelong struggle with feelings of inferiority and displacement; here, she displaces herself intentionally, leading to important lessons she learns about humanity while in the junkyard community

FALLING ACTION
Maya lives for a month in the junkyard with a group of homeless teenagers; she becomes San Francisco's first black streetcar conductor; she becomes pregnant; she graduates high school; she gives birth to a son and gains confidence

THEMES
Racism and segregation; debilitating displacement; resistance

MOTIFS
Strong black women; literature; naming

SYMBOLS
The Store; Maya's Easter dress

FORESHADOWING
The opening scene in the church foreshadows the struggles Maya will have to overcome in her life; when she cannot recite the poem and flees the church while crying and peeing, Angelou notes her fear of the people laughing at her and her sense of displacement and inferiority even among other blacks; she also leaves the church laughing, however, which foreshadows her ultimate success

Study Questions &
Essay Topics

Study Questions

1. *What is the significance of the opening scene of* I Know
Why the Caged Bird Sings?

The first lines of the book are two lines of a poem Maya tries to
recite in church on Easter Sunday: "What are you looking at me for?
I didn't come to stay . . ." These lines correspond to two main issues
she struggles with throughout her childhood: unhappiness with her
appearance and a perpetual feeling of displacement.

From an early age, Maya has been told that she is ugly both by
blacks, who notice the good looks of her brother and her parents, but
also by the racist American culture itself because her skin is dark and
her hair is kinky. In her fantasy, she sloughs off this unattractive
shell—a curse put on her by a jealous "fairy stepmother"—revealing
her true features: straight blond hair and blue eyes. Maya has been
fantasizing about the lavender taffeta dress Momma altered for her
and how in church she would look like one of the genteel white girls
whom everybody seemed to think of as perfect. But the dress's magic
fades as she sees it for what it is, a white woman's throwaway, and she
ends up self-conscious and humiliated.

With this opening scene Angelou encapsulates the struggles that
Maya will face in the years to come. Most black children in Stamps,
Arkansas, rarely had contact with white people because the segregation was so complete, yet at the age of five or six, Maya has already
internalized the idea that whiteness equals beauty. The opening
scene demonstrates the pervasive effects of racism on a black southern girl's consciousness. Although she is unaware, on an abstract
level, of her displacement in society, Maya has already begun to
regard her identity as a stigma.

Maya manages to escape the critical, mocking church community and laugh about her liberation, even though she knows she'll
get punished for it. Maya's escape foreshadows the fact that she
eventually overcomes the limitations of her childhood.

2.   *What is the significance of Maya's confrontation with Mrs. Cullinan?*

Maya's indignation when Mrs. Cullinan attempts to rename her Mary signals Maya's deepening sense of self-worth and race consciousness. Her subsequent rebellion—breaking the white woman's heirloom china—is a key moment in her development of a strong, positive sense of self. This renaming constitutes yet another form of displacement for Maya, and it reminds her of the renaming that occurs when white people use pejorative racial epithets in reference to blacks. Maya does not clarify whether she truly internalizes Mrs. Cullinan's renaming as a threat to her identity racially. Nevertheless, when Mrs. Cullinan presumptuously tries to determine Maya's name, Maya becomes furious and wishes to defend her identity.

Maya's reaction to Mrs. Cullinan exemplifies the subtler forms of resistance available to American blacks. According to social codes, Maya could not directly demand recognition of her identity, but she finds a subversive form of resistance. When Mrs. Cullinan yet again calls her Mary, Maya breaks some of her favorite dishes and then pretends that it was an accident, as Bailey recommended she do. Mrs. Cullinan drops her veneer of gentility and begins screaming racist remarks at Maya, showing the power of Maya's action to expose Mrs. Cullinan. Moreover, by switching back to Maya's original name, Mrs. Cullinan unwittingly relinquishes control over Maya and admits defeat. "Mary" is her property, but "Margaret" is not.

3. *What is the significance of the sermon delivered at the annual revival?*

The black southern church constituted another avenue for subversive resistance. At the revival, the preacher gives a sermon that criticizes white power without directly naming it. He never mentions white people, but his diatribe against greedy, self-righteous employers clearly attacks whites for paying miserable wages to black field laborers. He criticizes people who give charity with the expectation that the recipient will, in return, humble him or herself. He implicitly unleashes a diatribe against so-called charity from whites. Often, white people expected the black recipients of their charity to accept their lowly positions and avoid having pride in themselves. The people at the revival could entertain fantasies of their oppressors burning in hell with the support of divine will. For the most part, they shoulder the burden of their disadvantages of poverty and discrimination with resignation, attributing their suffering to God's will. However, on occasion, the black church provides an outlet for their smoldering anger.

4. *How does friendship with Louise change Maya?*

Maya's experiences prior to her first friendship—with Louise—mature her beyond her years. Before the rape, she is isolated, and after the rape, she becomes even more so. Moreover, she and Bailey grow apart as they each enters the turbulent years of adolescence. Maya moves largely in a world of adults—Mrs. Flowers, Momma, and Willie. With Louise, Maya begins to experience being a young girl for the first time. They speak inventive languages with each other. They hold hands and play in the forest, looking up at the sky like children. With Louise, Maya examines the question of young love and crushes on Valentine's Day. Their friendship is also Maya's first relationship that begins beyond the confines of her family. Perhaps symbolically, their friendship emerges when Maya ventures into the forest away from the fish fry to find a private place to pee.

5. ❧ *How did Maya's relationships with Big Bailey and Daddy Clidell differ? How does her relationship with Big Bailey compare with her relationship with Vivian?*

Big Bailey does not show respect for Maya. He likes to use her to distract his increasingly dissatisfied girlfriend, Dolores, contributing to the final explosion of animosity between Dolores and Maya. At first, Maya views Big Bailey as a handsome stranger, but in California she sees him as a man who is self-deceived. He works in the kitchen of a naval hospital but calls himself a medical dietitian. He speaks with proper English and puts on airs, but he lives in a trailer park and travels to Mexico to drink and sleep around. With the trip to Mexico, Big Bailey tries to show Maya a sphere where he feels empowered after having been disenfranchised for his entire life. Nevertheless, he becomes too drunk to see his daughter shining with pride over her accomplishment in the seat next to him on the way home. Moreover, he reacts selfishly to the confrontation between Maya and Dolores. He chooses to take Maya to a friend for treatment instead of a doctor because he wanted to avoid personal embarrassment. He does not want anyone to know that his girlfriend physically attacked his daughter.

Even though Daddy Clidell operates in a similarly lowbrow society—among con men and gamblers—he exhibits unquestionable respect both for Maya and for himself. She perceives him as a man of strength and tenderness, the ideal combination according to her. Moreover, Daddy Clidell laughs proudly when people think that Maya is his biological daughter. He has no insecurities to hide and no superiority to flaunt. As a result, he gives Maya affection and respect, unlike Big Bailey. Maya considers Daddy Clidell the first real father she has ever had. Similarly, even though Vivian also abandons her children at different points in the novel, she nevertheless contrasts with Big Bailey at the end of the novel. Vivian may live a melodramatic life associating in unsavory circles with gamblers and con men, but she represents power and unflinching honesty. She possesses the good qualities found in Big Bailey, like a wonderful sense of humor and a love for fun, but she complements these with a strong conscience and a deep respect for herself, Bailey, and Maya. Especially in the final chapters, Maya shows how she listens to her mother's wise words and sayings culled from her experiences.

SUGGESTED ESSAY TOPICS

1.   What characters serve as positive role models for Maya? Specifically, how does Maya come to her conclusions about the strength of black women?

2.   Does Maya's sense of displacement make her susceptible to Mr. Freeman's sexual advances? How does the rape and Mr. Freeman's death influence her throughout the rest of the book?

3.   Trace Maya's relationship with Bailey. Does it change significantly over the course of the book? Why or why not?

4.   What means of resistance against racism does Angelou depict? How did the opportunities for resistance for rural southern blacks differ from those available to the black people in San Francisco? How might they be attributed to a generational difference?

5.   Is Angelou a reliable narrator? To what extent does her own memory seem to distort her narrative? How would the significance of the work be different if it were fictional?

QUESTIONS & ESSAYS

REVIEW & RESOURCES

QUIZ

1. What is Maya Angelou's birth name?

   A. Margaret Ann Johnson
   B. Mary Ann Johnson
   C. Marguerite Ann Johnson
   D. Maya Ann Johnson

2. Why did Maya and Bailey's parents send them to Stamps, Arkansas?

   A. They had to move to St. Louis
   B. They had financial troubles
   C. Their grandmother needed company
   D. They got divorced

3. How did Maya and Bailey get to Stamps?

   A. By bus
   B. By train
   C. By car
   D. By plane

4. Why does Uncle Willie hide in the potato bin?

   A. Because he's crippled
   B. Because the police think he's a suspect in a crime
   C. Because there's a white lynch mob out looking for scapegoats
   D. Because he's afraid of ghosts

5. Who is the "most important person" in Maya's life?

   A. Bailey
   B. Momma
   C. Vivian
   D. Louise

6.   Which author is Maya's first love?

    A.   James Weldon Johnson
    B.   Henry Reed
    C.   William Shakespeare
    D.   Rudyard Kipling

7.   What does Momma do while the poor white children mock her in the yard?

    A.   Rake circles in the yard
    B.   Yell angrily
    C.   Hum a gospel tune
    D.   Weigh potatoes

8.   What does Maya do to defy Mrs. Cullinan?

    A.   She breaks her heirloom china
    B.   She tells her not to call her Mary
    C.   She refuses to go to work
    D.   She talks back to her guests

9.   Who is Maya's first friend?

    A.   Bertha
    B.   Vivian
    C.   Joyce
    D.   Louise

10.   What does Maya do for the first time in Mexico?

    A.   Drive a car
    B.   Drink a margarita
    C.   Sing in Spanish
    D.   Get angry with her father

11.   Why does Bailey stay late at the movies?

    A.   Because he loses track of time
    B.   Because the actress reminds him of his mother
    C.   Because he is afraid of the dark
    D.   Because Joyce made him

12. Who rapes Maya?

   A. Big Bailey
   B. Daddy Clidell
   C. Uncle Willy
   D. Mr. Freeman

13. Where does Maya live after running away from her father's friend's house?

   A. A garage
   B. A junkyard
   C. A shelter
   D. A friend's house

14. Which famous figure sustains black pride for those who congregate at the Store?

   A. Martin Luther King, Jr.
   B. Joe Louis
   C. Booker T. Washington
   D. Michael Jordan

15. How does Vivian make a living?

   A. By working in gambling parlors
   B. By working in hospitals
   C. By working as a streetcar conductor
   D. By working as a waitress

16. Why does Maya stop talking?

   A. Because she only likes to read
   B. Because Grandmother Baxter hits her
   C. Because she feels the devil will come out of her if she talks
   D. Because Mr. Freeman rapes her

17. What does Grandfather Baxter teach his sons to be?

   A. Kind
   B. Thieves
   C. Con men
   D. Mean

18. In which city does Maya feel she belongs?

    A.   St. Louis
    B.   New York
    C.   San Francisco
    D.   Los Angeles

19. Why does Maya sleep with the neighborhood boy?

    A.   Because she is in love with him
    B.   To prove she is not gay
    C.   To make Bailey mad
    D.   Because she's bored

20. What does Maya hide from Vivian and Daddy Clidell?

    A.   Her pregnancy
    B.   Her job
    C.   Her boyfriend
    D.   Her trip to Mexico

21. Whom does Maya consider a real father figure?

    A.   Uncle Willy
    B.   Mr. Freeman
    C.   Big Bailey
    D.   Daddy Clidell

22. What does Maya do before she slaps Dolores?

    A.   She warns her
    B.   She does a little dance
    C.   She gives her the middle finger
    D.   She scratches the car

23. Who makes Maya feel like an equal human being?

    A.   Mr. Donleavy
    B.   Miss Kirwin
    C.   Dr. Lincoln
    D.   Mrs. Cullinan

24. Blacks replace what ethnic minority in San Francisco during World War II?

    A. Japanese
    B. Germans
    C. Chinese
    D. Italians

25. What breakthrough does Maya achieve in San Francisco?

    A. She becomes the first black student in her high school
    B. She becomes the first black streetcar conductor
    C. She becomes the first black valedictorian
    D. She becomes the first black bus driver

SUGGESTIONS FOR FURTHER READING

BARNES, MARIAN E. AND GOSS, LINDA. *Talk That Talk: An Anthology of African-American Storytelling.* New York: Simon and Schuster, 1989.

BLOOM, HAROLD. *Maya Angelou.* Broomall, Pennsylvania: Chelsea House Publishers, 2001.

BRAXTON, JOANNE M. I KNOW WHY THE CAGED BIRD SINGS: *A Casebook.* New York: Oxford University Press, 1999.

COURTNEY-CLARKE, MARGARET. *Maya Angelou: The Poetry of Living.* New York: C. Potter, 1999.

HAGEN, LYMAN B. *Heart of a Woman, Mind of a Writer, and Soul of a Poet: A Critical Analysis of the Writings of Maya Angelou.* Lanham, Maryland: University Press of America, 1996.

LUPTON, MARY JANE. *Maya Angelou: A Critical Companion.* Westport, Connecticut: Greenwood Press, 1998.

MEGNA-WALLACE, JOANNE. *Understanding* I KNOW WHY THE CAGED BIRD SINGS: *A Student Casebook to Issues, Sources, and Historical Documents.* Westport, Connecticut: Greenwood Press, 1998.

WILLIAMS, MARY E., editor. *Readings on Maya Angelou.* San Diego, California: Greenhaven Press, 1997.

A Note on the Type

The typeface used in SparkNotes study guides is Sabon, created by master typographer Jan Tschichold in 1964. Tschichold revolutionized the field of graphic design twice: first with his use of asymmetrical layouts and sanserif type in the 1930s when he was affiliated with the Bauhaus, then by abandoning assymetry and calling for a return to the classic ideals of design. Sabon, his only extant typeface, is emblematic of his latter program: Tschichold's design is a recreation of the types made by Claude Garamond, the great French typographer of the Renaissance, and his contemporary Robert Granjon. Fittingly, it is named for Garamond's apprentice, Jacques Sabon.

SPARKNOTES
TEST PREPARATION
GUIDES

The SparkNotes team figured it was time to cut standardized tests down to size. We've studied the tests for you, so that SparkNotes test prep guides are:

Smarter:
Packed with critical-thinking skills and test-
taking strategies that will improve your score.

Better:
Fully up to date, covering all new features of the tests,
with study tips on every type of question.

Faster:
Our books cover exactly what you need to
know for the test. No more, no less.

SparkNotes Study Guides: